THE
COURAGEOUS
COMMONER

THE

COURAGEOUS

COMMONER

A BIOGRAPHY

OF

ANDREW JOHNSON

By

B. CARROLL REECE

EDUCATION FOUNDATION, INC.
Charleston, West Virginia
1962

Manufactured in the United States of America

PREFACE

Reared as I was, in a history-haunted section of the United States made forever great by the footsteps and activities of such men as Daniel Boone, David Crockett, Sam Houston, Captain John Sevier, Andrew Jackson, and others, it may seem strange that Andrew Johnson was one of the giants of my boyhood.

The explanation is simple. Johnson lived and struggled, married and died within a few miles of my own birthplace. The far-flung panorama of the Great Smoky Mountains, with their summits cloaked in blue mist, fascinated him just as much as it always has fascinated me. His people are my people and their ways are my ways.

From the lips of men and women who knew Johnson, I learned the story of his life and the true worth in which he was held by those who knew him—those among whom he walked, lived, and died. Many years ago, I determined to do some day what I could to make my fellow Americans see the real Andrew Johnson whom we know down in East Tennessee—the man who put the country above self and who dared his enemies to do their worst.

Many Americans, because of distorted history, still believe that Andrew Johnson was a drunken opportunist whom Lincoln's death thrust into an office from which he was soon impeached.

Abraham Lincoln frequently defended him for his sacrifices for the Nation, and Lincoln and Stanton both asked the same question of the country: "What man in America has done more for the Nation's life than Andrew Johnson?"

In the course of my years on Capitol Hill as a representative from Johnson's former district in Tennessee, it became my pleasure to introduce the bill which made his old home a national historical monument.

It has been in the last fifteen years that scholarly historians have given readers a more honest picture of

Andrew Johnson. However, I have always felt that such historians failed to make the general reader understand the real man and explain his motivations which caused his rise from the humblest of origins to the highest office in the land.

With that thought in view, I have spent endless hours browsing through his private papers and all that I could find written or printed about him and his times. The result is this biography; it is neither fictionalized nor, it is fervently hoped, encumbered by scholarly argument so that the courageous commoner may be understood by those whom he loved and served—the people.

CONTENTS

HONORABLE B. CARROLL REECE
(See biography, page 161)

MRS. B. CARROLL REECE
(See biography, page 163)

CHAPTER 1

INTRODUCTION: DEMIGOD OR MORTAL?

Andrew Johnson, seventeenth president of the United States, stood with bared head in a little, vine-covered summerhouse on a tiny eminence at the Soldier's Home, in Washington, overlooking the National Cemetery.

Before him, and on either side, stretched row upon row of little white tombstones, marking the graves of Union soldiers, lately fallen in the titanic struggle between the states. It was a tragic spectacle, for the rows seemed endless and uncountable. It was late afternoon of the fall day in 1868, and the setting sun seemed caressingly to gild the myriad stones. Far in the background, blue shadows were silhouetting the Maryland hills.

With brooding eyes, Johnson stared silently at the scene for many minutes. He had not been feeling well of late and his Secretary of the Navy, Gideon Welles, had urged him to take a few hours off that afternoon.

The cemetery was not the proper spot for the relaxation he so desperately needed. Few men on earth had ever shouldered burdens such as he had borne; few men had ever carried on despite such treachery of associates, calumny, castigation, and abuse.

The sad spectacle of these acres of gravestones was not conducive to placid thoughts. Perhaps he was to blame for them, if one wanted to look at things from the ground up.

He remembered back to that terrible day in December, 1860, when the hesitant northern members of Congress had been prepared to break up the Union and let the seceding southern states go their way in peace rather than sanction force.

A solitary, lonely figure, he had risen to his feet, and with amazing eloquence had thundered the words which fought against the division of the Union.

1

Such words had helped to touch off the Civil War. When he had finished speaking, every man seemed to know his course.

The acres before him marked the last resting place of thousands who had believed in him and his credo. Throughout the land were other places like these.

The vagaries of fate, however, had demanded greater sacrifices of him than blood or merciful death. From him it had exacted years of pain and ignominy that were to last all his life. Time and again, mobs had sought him out for lynching. Again and again he had been hanged in effigy. For years, he had been hounded like a beast of prey, separated from his family and friends, a constant target for assassins.

His family! A half-smile flickered across his set, grim face as he recalled that long-ago day when he had trudged into Greeneville, a dirty, barefooted, poverty-stricken young tailor, about to meet the courageous girl whose influence was to guide him to the very presidency.

Eliza McCardle! Beautiful, old-fashioned, noble Eliza! She was a living martyr to the strange destiny which had led him to the presidency. Her terrible sufferings and deprivations during the War had afflicted her with incurable consumption.

But for her help and belief it was doubtful that he could have risen above his trade as a tailor. She had taught him to write and to enjoy good reading. Patiently, she had undertaken to help him overcome his lack of schooling. With never a complaint she had stood by him through days and trials that would have broken most women. She had winced when men had dubbed him illegitimate. She had given courage during those hideous days of his military governorship of Tennessee. She suffered when petty men and political opponents, jealous of his power, had dubbed him a drunkard, for she had known better. When they had tried impeachment, these little, scorpion-tongued mediocrities, her faith had been all he needed. Truly, but for Eliza and his own great pride and sureness that he was right, he would have given up long ago.

The tombstones must have blurred and wavered in his

vision. His past life seemed to unroll before him like some living, pulsating panorama. It was almost unbelievable that he, a poor widow's son, should today be President of the United States!

But he was, and God knows the way had not been easy or always clear sailing. His past sped by in swift review — tailor — alderman — state legislator — governor — representative in Congress — senator — military governor — vice-president and now president. How simple it sounded! But only he and Eliza knew the true story of the years.

He had committed many personal mistakes in those forty-odd years of the struggle but, nevertheless, he could plainly see that in one thing alone he had never wavered or stumbled—every move he had made had been with the unselfish thought of serving his people and his country. Never had he given a second thought to self. Never had he allowed selfish considerations or party obligations to interfere with what he considered his duty to the Union.

Lincoln's plans for reconstruction and his own ideas had never been given a fair chance. The South was still stricken and prostrate. Election time was rolling around again and the country was more divided than ever before.

His enemies had attempted to impeach him. It had been a ghastly mistake on the part of those who argued they had the country's best interests at heart. It would slow up peaceful reconstruction, curtail business recovery, cost many lives, and sow endless seeds of hate. But for his own personal courage, it might well have touched off another Civil War. Thousands of former soldiers as well as officers had wired, written, and personally begged him to use force on the Radicals who had hamstrung his efforts to effect recovery. Many of the writers were hotheaded, and it had been a struggle to keep them calm and convince them everything would come out all right. Eliza had assured him of that. But, for that matter, everything was going to come out right. It had to. Behind the treachery and greed of associates and the stupidity of nitwits, he knew the law of life was progression and never retrogression.

Abruptly he turned on his heel and strode to the waiting horses. William Crooks, his Secret Service bodyguard,

3

trudged after him and helped him into the saddle. They trotted back to the White House over the dusty, heavily rutted roads.

As they neared the stately, yet shabby old mansion, Johnson held back his steed until the guard was abreast. "Crooks!" he exclaimed in a strange burst of confidence, "everybody misunderstands me. I haven't been trying to introduce anything new. I was only trying to carry out the measures towards the South that Mr. Lincoln would have done had he lived."[1]

If one reads everything available on the life and time of Andrew Johnson—spends days, weeks, months, and even years, among all the millions of words and the great mass of material pertaining to those days, one cannot escape the conclusion in that voluminous record of fact, fancy, and hate. Here was a man predestined to serve his country in the hours of her greatest need!

Men were never neutral over the subject of this tailor of Greeneville. They were either his bitter enemies or his faithful friends. Candor compells the admission that he had more enemies than friends, although in the darkest hours of his life, countless thousands eagerly offered to fight for him and his principles.

It is a lamentable fact that so few of his real friends left worthwhile records and impressions of him for historians and posterity to study; whereas, his enemies left endless material so derogatory as to bewilder and confuse the fairest-minded student.

Therefore, it is still a simpler task to follow the lead of his enemies rather than to interpret Johnson and his stand for rehabilitating the Union. Thus, we are presented with the recent re-evaluations.

Until about 1905, when the Library of Congress acquired Johnson's private papers[2] and other personal records, it was customary for historians to speak of him in the worst possible terms. With those papers made available, historians like James Schouler and Clifton R. Hall, and biographers like Robert W. Winston, George Fort Milton, and Lloyd Paul Stryker, gave us a new picture of one of America's most badly misunderstood men. Yet ask the

4

average person who Johnson was and they are quite apt to say: "Let me see, wasn't he the president who was impeached?" Others may even assure you he was illegitimate and a terrible drunkard.

Nothing could be more unfair to him. His enemies brought impeachment proceedings against him but didn't succeed. As for his paternity, it seems to be impeccable. All the women possessed wedding certificates. Tales of his drinking were the result of cowardly machinations by his enemies. Unable to break his proud spirit and determination in any other way, they resorted to calumny and character assassination to defeat him. They spoke in terms which today would earn disgrace instead of power.

Biographers have helped to spread this hymn of hate against one who was every inch as great as Lincoln or Washington in his services to the Nation and the cause of the common man. Charnwood wrote: "Lincoln could not bear the sight of him." This is nonsense. Even novelists have found it expedient to belittle Johnson as they pretend great knowledge of the times of which they have written. The record proves otherwise.

Men couldn't comprehend him because fate set him a task to do. That task was to hold this Nation together, through hell and high water. He accomplished the task because he was indomitable, bullheaded, fiery, afraid of no man. He wouldn't accept advice because the problem was too simple to require advice; it was merely one of suppressing greed and keeping the Union intact. His stubbornness in his course was his greatest political failure. He did fail to reckon with humanity, which is not simple but complex. He was "unpolitical" to a fault. But his stubbornness was on the other hand his greatest virtue. He did soften the radical blows on the South with his vetoes. The South, wrong in his eyes from the outset, in bringing on the war, was, after the war had ended, nonetheless American and still an integral part of this Union to which cause thousands and Abraham Lincoln had been sacrificed. In the end, Johnson triumphed. He was not a figure in Greek tragedy—the strong man pitted against ill fate. Returning to the Senate, in 1875, unscathed by the cor-

5

ruption of his time, he became the symbol of union in the eyes of the people, and he died in that year when the Nation had rejected the radicals and former opponents were once again rebuilding for peace.

CHAPTER 2

"AS THE TREE INCLINETH"

Who was this man, Andrew Johnson, to be thrown into a seething cauldron of civil conflict? What kind of man would sacrifice himself in such a manner? To such questions, the years of his youth perhaps provide the answers.

"I think of Andrew Johnson as of a strong and sturdy pine in the forest, which has grown up distorted by some rocky obstruction, twisted out of shape and crooked in the trunk, and yet vigorous at the core. He was stubborn in political opinions where he thought himself right, defiant, ready to fight for them; yet those opinions were just, enlightened and such as only a sound and independent statesman could have formed. Congress wished in that promoted Vice President a compliant Executive and found a constructive one instead."[3] So wrote James Schouler, the historian who knew Johnson personally.

Finding almost insurmountable obstructions in Johnson's life—obstructions that shaped, influenced, or even twisted his life—is a simple matter. But for those impediments he might never have become the great man he was.

Poverty was the early formative handicap of his life. He rose above it, but, nevertheless, it left a mark that was stamped on almost his every adult action. It soured his boyhood and narrowed his viewpoint. It made him hate privileged classes, and he never ceased to fight them.

Born in Raleigh, North Carolina, in the early evening of December 29, 1808, in a tiny cottage near the stables of a popular inn of the day, Andy was quickly compelled to realize there were two strata of society and that he and his belonged to the lower one. "Mudsills" was the cynical definition wished upon the "poor whites" by Senator Hammond, and the word became a battle cry with Johnson all his life.

7

Being a "mudsill" meant one was too poor to attain an education, learn a profession, own a farm, or do much of anything except menial labor. It meant one was always looked down upon by the other stratum—the so-called aristocrats. That division of class soured the growing boy's soul. It was responsible for some of his greatest forensic battles. Never in his life did he fail to take up the gauntlet of battle for the "mudsills" against the landed gentry. The Homestead Bill which he fathered and fought for so many years undoubtedly owes its genesis to his sympathetic concern for others of humble origin.

Johnson was barely three years old when his father, a popular, hard-working man of no education, saved the lives of two drunken aristocrats from drowning. Exposure and exhaustion put him to bed, and he died within a month. The local newspaper eulogized his sacrifice and his life in the community and they buried him under a tablet memoralizing his heroism.

That tablet didn't help the poor widow with two young sons. There is no record to indicate that the two wealthy rescued persons ever did a thing to aid the widow, save to indenture Bill, the older boy, as an apprentice in 1814. That helped a little but it was not enough. One may be sure of the effect those adolescent years had on a youth whom fate was to one day make President of the United States. One can imagine what his thoughts were, living amidst abject poverty, in a community of many wealthy people.

When Andrew was fourteen, his mother could bear no more. She bound Andy to one James Selby, a tailor. Bill's master, Colonel Henderson, died about this time, and so Selby took on both boys, as tailor apprentices. Mrs. Johnson, desperately trying to better her lonely lot, remarried and it proved a poor venture.[4]

Living on table scraps, forced to toil long hours, and made to wear cheap homespun "because he was so hard on clothes," young Andy glumly looked about him. It was unjust that some children were able to go to school, engage freely in all sorts of games, live in fine homes, and apparently have no worries. It was unfair that he and his brother and the regular tailors were forever making fine clothing from

8

Tailor Shop owned by Andrew Johnson at Greeneville, Tennessee

Monument to Andrew Johnson, erected by the United States Government

ANDREW JOHNSON
17th President of the United States (1865-69)

Home of Andrew Johnson at Greeneville, Tennessee

imported materials for men who never worked. Rebellion was being born in Andy's soul.[5]

The foreman of the shop, one Litchford, and Dr. Hill, of the town, took pity on the boy. They undertook to teach him the alphabet during spare moments. Dr. Hill, dropping into the shop whenever possible, read from the newspapers and several books of famous speeches. These speeches made great impressions on the young apprentice. He learned some of them by heart. Dr. Hill, a kindly man and somewhat of an orator, gave him lessons in the art of public speaking. To encourage him in trying to read, the doctor made him a present of several of the little books. It wasn't long before they said Andy's voice "will carry further than a city block."[6]

The long hours of confinement and the seeds of knowledge being implanted into his mind brought about revolt. Two years later, after a minor escapade, Andy and his brother took "French" leave and were duly posted as "runaways" with a ten-dollar reward on their heads.

At the tender age of sixteen, Andy opened up a little shop of his own in Carthage, seventy-five miles away from home. Naturally, it was foredoomed to failure. What the townspeople thought about so young and poverty-stricken a tailor is not a matter of record, and perhaps it is just as well. A few months later, he and Bill were trying their luck in Laurens, South Carolina. Things were no better there. There he experienced a minor love affair which has received more publicity than deserved. Puppy love, it made sensational reading in newspapers and a national magazine after his death.[7]

As a matter of fact, Johnson had but one love affair in his life and that was with the woman he married—Eliza McCardle. It is unfortunate that our literature has never been enriched with the full story of this remarkable woman and the amazing part she played in sweetening his life and keeping him headed for his goal.

Judge Robert Winston, William Crooks, and a few others have given us clear pictures of the part Eliza McCardle played in Johnson's life but there is still much of her story that has never been told.

Andy and Eliza met by chance one late afternoon in September, 1826. Ragged, barefoot, dusty and dirty from a month's travel, young Andrew was leading a little caravan into Greeneville, Tennessee. The caravan consisted of his mother, his indigent stepfather, Turner Dougherty, and his brother, Bill. All their goods were piled into a rude, two-wheeled cart drawn by an old horse.

Despairing of ever getting a start in Raleigh, or even the State of North Carolina, Andrew had talked his family into making the long trip to Tennessee. He had already made a visit to the state, having spent some six months working for a tailor in Rutledge and Columbia. He might have stayed there but a letter came from his mother describing her unhappy marital woes. So, he had walked back to Raleigh and persuaded them to leave for good.

The arduous trip over the Smokies took almost a month. They followed the trail of Daniel Boone, already famous for almost half a century. It was an ordeal but Johnson never regretted it for a moment. Greeneville hadn't been planned for a destination but fate made it so.

As they entered the town, eager for rest and a meal, Andy paused before a group of girls just leaving Rhea Academy, of which he was later to be elected to the board. Of a hazel-eyed, brown-haired, vivacious girl, he inquired where they might camp or rent a cottage. It was Eliza, seventeen-year-old daughter of a widow. History has it that Eliza sent him to the Blue Gum Spring to camp and then, more in earnest than jest, told her laughing companions, "There goes my beau, girls, mark it."[8]

They were married the following spring, and by a strange coincidence the ceremony was performed by Mordecai Lincoln who later served on the Board of Aldermen with him. Andrew was barely nineteen, and she was but eighteen. They lived and worked in a two-room cottage. The front room served as Andy's tailor shop and the fountainhead of his future political triumphs. The back room comprised in one the kitchen, parlor, and bedroom for the happy young couple.

There little Martha Johnson was born, afterwards destined to be mistress of the White House during her mother's

10

lingering illness of tuberculosis. There, too, was born Charles, merry-hearted and convivial. Of a sudden, Johnson's life changed from gloom to happiness. He prospered. Men liked him, and they liked his work. He bought a little farm for his mother and stepfather near the city. Brother Bill, however, soon headed for Texas, drawn by the banner of Sam Houston.

A new world now opened up to Andrew. Eliza set about the task of teaching him. He could already spell a little and read, but "big" words were beyond him, and he was rather uncouth. Eliza had endless patience with her rugged but apt pupil, however. Already, few could equal him in argument, but only time and experience were to bring him logic.

The tailor shop became a mecca for the backwoods politicians of the day and the humble mechanics of the town.[9]

Johnson's surroundings were an irrepressible factor in his development. Eastern Tennessee at this time was largely populated by a strangely independent, aggressive, lion-hearted people who were mainly of Scotch-Irish stock. Most of them had pushed up from Virginia and Carolina Piedmont. They hated class domination. They despised any and all artificiality.

Few of them had ever found life anything but a hard and constant struggle for the simplest things. Most of them had arrived in the section as humble pioneers in search of land and an opportunity to eke out a living and rear a family. Their possessions were simple, their lives were similarly so. They were God-fearing, loyal, and brave to the point of foolhardiness. The region being largely hills and mountains, with heavy forests everywhere and rich river bottoms alternating with rugged coves or valleys, there was a natural tendency to clannishness. For roads and trails were few and strangers more so. Neighbors stood by each other, asking only that the other man was sound in his opinions.

The result of all this was a simple democratic society, where men took their politics seriously. Independent, they wanted to be ruled as little as possible and taxed the same

11

way. Although food was plentiful albeit simple, luxuries were few and far between. Andrew Jackson's thinking gripped the section where so much of his earlier manhood had been spent. Men prided themselves on being Jacksonian Democrats.

Johnson was not the least of Jacksonian enthusiasts. He had been named for "Old Hickory" as an infant and throughout his life he regarded Jackson as a kind of patron saint. Many of his political theories were those of the hero of New Orleans. Jackson studied his career with interest and wrote him a few letters of encouragement—letters Johnson valued as no other possession.

To many people of Tennessee, Johnson was, in fact, considered a veritable reincarnation of Jackson and, in time, others throughout the entire country shared this feeling. Scores of letters have been preserved[10] commenting on the similarity in their viewpoints. George Fort Milton summed it up nicely in a single sentence, "Old Hickory was Andrew Johnson's political pilot, the model of his conduct and the idol of his heart."[11]

With a growing prosperity and a contented marital life, Johnson found himself firmly rooted in the community life of Greeneville. More and more he was drawn to the humble people and of them to himself. He grew to accept their ideals and virtues. Half frontier, partly western and southern, the community was fertile soil for a man filled with the lust of life and imbued with ambitions. It was a community where fidelity to purpose or particular principles was the cardinal virtue. In Johnson's case, this was evidenced by his love for the Union, and because he was consistent, eastern Tennessee forever stood by him.

His shop was fast becoming the center of Greene County democratic politics. Almost daily, he hired a young student to read famous speeches or essays, and as he and his men plied their needles or irons, one and all were learning Jefferson's speeches, *Elliot's Debates,* and the Constitution of the United States by heart. Saturday nights always saw a throng assembled there, arguing over the topics of the day or still vying over the result of the regular Friday night debating class held at nearby Tusculum College, the oldest

12

college west of the Alleghenies. There had been another debating class at Greeneville College but this had gone out of existence.

This college debating society entailed the walking of eight miles—four out and four back—but Johnson gladly tramped the night road once or twice a week. He was lifelong unquenchably athirst for knowledge, like most self-educated men.

These debates and the weekly get-together in his shop were developing Johnson as a speaker of note and a leader of his set. Neither profound nor adroit, his mind moved in a straightaway. He would find the core of a subject and then hammer away until every auditor knew it by heart.[12]

It was natural that this village leadership and this new-found gift of words would lead to something. Impressed by his ideals and ability, a little group of new-found friends elected him a town alderman in 1829, much to the chagrin of the aristocrats. In 1830, he was re-elected. As a sort of birthday present, his friends made him town mayor on his twenty-first anniversary. He held this post for three successive terms, no small honor for one who was little more than a youth. An extra laurel was handed him in 1832, when, at the tender age of twenty-three, he was appointed a trustee of Rhea College.

The outcome of these local political triumphs was obvious. He decided to dedicate his whole life to public service. He ran for the state legislature. His opponent was Major Matthew Stephenson, wealthy socialite. The Major succumbed to Andrew's brutal forensic onslaughts. To Nashville went the tailor.

Green and untried, he made more than one sorry mistake in those early days, but the people stayed with him. They saw that he had their best interests at heart. He was violently opposed to public debt, higher taxation, and any and all class legislation. He fought the chartering of a railroad by the state on the Jacksonian grounds that it created a public monopoly. He caused opposition in high places, the consequence of which was his defeat after a bitter campaign wherein Johnson's behavior was to foreshadow his activities in the Congressional campaigns of 1866.

13

In 1839, however, he won re-election and supported Van Buren's candidacy for the presidency.

In 1840, Johnson was chosen one of the Democratic electors from the state at large. The outcome of this was his election as a state senator. By 1843, he was on his way to Washington as Congressman from his district. Here, for the first time in his young life, he found that if he wanted success "he must be seen and not heard" until he had served his novitiate. Otherwise, such a young representative might commit some blunder and ruin his career.

Johnson held his tongue and ran again and had little trouble convincing his constituents that he was their most suitable representative. In truth, he was. During this second term, March 27, 1846, he introduced his famous Homestead Bill. Behind its creation was his lifelong interest in his fellow "mudsills" and how to aid them get a start in life.

The Homestead Bill was political dynamite. Nine new territories in the West were struggling for admission to the Union as states. Filled with new settlers with potential voting power, they would come to Congress with doubts about slavery, particularly its extension to their areas. The South feared them. Definitely, southern leaders were opposed to free homesteads and new northern states. Thus the issue, dragging on for years, was fiercely championed by Johnson.[13]

His long struggle in the House for his Homestead Bill —six years and two months—also gained him the enmity of Thad Stevens and Jefferson Davis, both of whom were violently opposed to it.[13] Johnson tread warily. His bill might doom slavery and as a southerner by birth and a representative of a slave state, also owning ten slaves himself, his position was almost paradoxical. May 12, 1852, however, he succeeded in having the bill passed in the House.

There the bill was doomed to linger, while around it and over it gathered the slowly darkening clouds of civil war. In the Southland, Johnson became the focal point for abuse. But in the North his star was beginning to rise. He was invited everywhere to make speeches. Southern newspapers began to cudgel him; southern Whigs to fear him. It was time to do something to this dangerous upstart.

14

The method employed was simple and direct, but debatable as to what was really gained. Although Tennessee was now practically Democratic, the state legislature was almost entirely controlled by Whigs. Calmly, yet with malice aforethought, the legislature gerrymandered the state. Johnson's home county of Greene was cut off from the First District and attached to the Second which was overwhelmingly Whig. In disgust, Johnson came home in 1852. His "swan song" to the House was quaint and picturesque. "Our General Assembly has parted my garments and are now casting lots for my vesture, but there is much in the future!"[14]

How much the future held was unknown at the moment to Johnson. He was hurt, mortified, and angry. He planned to retire from public life. His letters home and to his friends indicate how crushed he was.[14] But, the home-going brought new green fields.

Governor W. B. Campbell, the Whig governor of the state, suddenly refused a third term and his rejection of the honor brought consternation to the party, for he was their strongest man. In despair, they fell back on the gentleman who had maneuvered the Tailor out of office, Gustavus A. Henry, noted far and wide as the "Eagle Orator."

This was Andrew Johnson's opportunity, and the state rallied to his support. Hailed as "the man of the people and the people's man," he was promptly endorsed by more counties than any other Democratic candidate. In the pre-election speeches that followed, he proceeded to pluck the "Eagle's" wings in the most boisterous, sardonic [*sardonic*] campaign that Tennessee had ever seen. "I'll 'Henrymander' him!" cried Johnson to the gleeful electors.[15]

The "eagle" soared no more. Andrew Johnson became Governor of Tennessee, receiving great majorities from middle Tennessee, and on October 17, 1853, he entered office —the first governor to give his entire time to that state leadership. As a disciple of Jefferson and Jackson, he made gubernatorial history in that he set out to help the common man. His success was a terrible blow to the Whigs for in it they read the death knell of their party. When, to their

15

consternation, he offered himself for re-election, they stopped at nothing in their efforts to defeat him. They aligned with the Know-Nothing party and the campaign that followed has few equals in political history—villification from start to finish, marked by brawls with bowie knife and pistol, which ended more than one of the stirring sixty debates entered into by Johnson and Meredith P. Gentry, his opponent.

Johnson won. The state was never to forget his statement in his inaugural speech: "The people have never deserted me and, God being willing, I will never desert them."

Similar to Jackson, he followed the role of strong executive, and in contrast to reconstruction days, he worked relatively well with his legislature, despite the fact that he suffered with a Whig Senate. To aid the mechanics, a class which always had his interest, he attempted the removal of the state prison to some central point where the inmates would produce iron so that prisoner craftsmanship could not compete with free labor. The legislature balked.

His opinions were far more notable than his successes or failures and indicated sound judgment and balance in his leadership. He advocated reduction of high tax on the merchants' right to do business; he wanted a reform in state banking, and the judiciary, which demonstrated Jeffersonian influence; and he cautioned moderation in the acceptance and use of Federal funds by the state, but he was instrumental in putting such money to use for the construction of sound roads, which included aid to several railroad builders. To bring improvement to farming methods, an Agricultural Bureau was established.

Johnson administratively was outstanding principally for measures to aid education. A State Library and Office of the Librarian were created. That Library today is among the Nation's best.

For several years the common folk of Tennessee desired a system of tax-supported common schools. Repeatedly the legislation had been defeated by the Whigs, supported by aristocratic merchants and planters. But with a "people's Champion" in office, the time was ripe for victory. Nudged by Johnson's urgent appeals, after much debate, the House and Senate passed a bill to establish a system of common schools which provided a 25c levy on each poll and a 2½ per cent tax on each $100 of taxable property. Money thus collected was distributed to the counties.

During the closing weeks of Johnson's first term, the *Daily Union and American* of March 7, 1854, commented that: "Rarely if ever, has there been a more harmonious session of the Legislature, in this State, and certainly never one which has transacted more important business. That Johnson exhibited excellent abilities as an executive. . ." under normal circumstances, there can be no doubt. His work as Governor evidences further the great lies about his incapabilities which the Radicals of Reconstruction days heaped upon him.

In that second term, Johnson did much to liquidate an old and heavy state indebtedness. It was also his lifelong pride that, through him, the state acquired the Hermitage, residence and tomb of Andrew Jackson, lately deceased.[16]

By now, thanks to his endorsement and campaign services to Buchanan, Johnson had become a national figure in Democratic politics. People spoke of him as "Old Andy" and he was the idol of the masses, trusting them and being trusted in turn.

Not wishing to accept a third term as governor, it was obvious where Andrew Johnson's road was leading. An opportunity existing, the Democratic state legislature promptly sent him to Washington as Senator.

The illiterate "bound boy of Raleigh," the Tailor of Greeneville, had grown mighty and a power to reckon with. He hurried to Washington to keep his rendezvous with fate.

CHAPTER 3

THIS WAS HIS FINEST HOUR

How had Senator Johnson helped to bring on the Civil War, a thought which had passed through his mind that day in the cemetery in 1868? On December 18, 1860, he had set the Nation on its course, one which Lincoln himself was to pursue. In the dark hour of secession and confusion, he cried out to preserve the Union.

On December 18, in the Nation's Capitol, a scene unfolded that defied description. Pandemonium raged like a contagion in the otherwise dignified portals of the United States Senate. The flickering gaslights, bordering the skylight in the great chamber, shed a weird illumination down over galleries packed and jammed with vociferous, uncontrolled spectators whose catcalls, cheers, jeers, and groans ofttimes drowned out the bedlam of voices rising from the chamber floor itself.

The Senators from South Carolina had triumphantly announced the Palmetto State was withdrawing from the Union and, what is more, wanted her share of the national wealth, forgetting in their rage there might also be such a thing as a share in a national debt. Noisily endorsing this move, the representatives of her sister states proclaimed their readiness to join hands and fight to the bitter end.

The roar of voices from wildly angry men mocked all parliamentary procedure. Pistols had been drawn, epithets hurled, and more than one challenge to a duel made. The flickering lights caught the reflection of opened dirks. One historian even records hearing the sound of blades clicking open and shut during lulls that afternoon as nervous owners fingered them.

Northern leaders were confused and hesitant during those tragic hours. All too long, these hot-tempered, easily ruffled southern colleagues had worried them with their readiness to fight when debate waxed too warm or became overly personal. More than once, timid members had introduced resolutions forbidding the carrying of concealed weapons on the Senate floor. Today seemed to mark the end of everything for which wise men had argued.

"Let the South do what it wishes!" shouted more than one northern pacifist. "Let her leave and good riddance to her!" echoed others. A few tried to stand their ground, but their frenzied appeals were lost in the uproar.

Senator Lane, of Oregon, former soldier in the Mexican War and ardently southern in feelings and views by reason of birth, added new fuel to the conflagration of hatred by giving away the chief reason for the rising bitterness and desire for secession.

"Lincoln's election is unconstitutional!" he bellowed. "It should be voided! It should go before the Supreme Court! It is unthinkable that a sectional president should be elected on a sectional platform."[17]

Northern members roared with derision. Hale, of New Hampshire, somehow got the floor and, in a bull-like voice that reached every nook and cranny of the room, vehemently cried: "If the people's will expressed by a constitutional election will not be submitted to and war is the alternative, then LET IT COME!"

From the galleries rose a mighty sound of hissing. It was like a giant wave about to break and it was so ominous that members flinched as they stared upward. Vainly the speaker pounded for order. His gavel shattered to pieces, and he tossed the handle aside in his despair. What was order in this bedlam? Order was something that seemed gone forever. The Union was coming to an end, so why worry any more!

A new sound suddenly filled the room. It seemed to shake the very skylights and make the gas jets flicker as it drowned out lesser noises. It was the high-pitched, scornful voice of Wigfall, the fiery Texan.

"Coerce the South? Bah! Try it and we will welcome you to the harvest of death! Future generations will

19

point to a small hillock upon our borders showing the reception we have given you!"[18]

On and on, flowed his tirade of threat and sarcasm, his every sentence punctuated with the wild approval of excited sympathizers in the tiers above him and from all sides.

"Sirs! We will no longer submit. I tell you cotton is king and there is no crowned head in Europe that does not bow the knee in fealty. I tell you of the North if you wish to live long in our company you must abolish your so-called liberty laws, abolish your abolition societies and all newspapers advocating abolition!"[19]

Andrew Johnson, seated near Jefferson Davis, soon to become president of the Confederacy, listened as long and as silently as he could. Beyond all men present, he saw that someone had to speak now and say the right words. Well did he know that on the shoulders of that speaker rested a terrible burden; that abuse, castigation, threats, challenges, and even death might be his fate.

The Tennesseean was like a man in a trance. Behind him, as if looking backward down a high hill, he saw his whole life stretched out like a road across a plain. Now he understood his past struggles—now he understood what life expected from him. This might be the Mt. Nebo of his career but he mustn't falter; mustn't fail. With strange insight, he even realized why his reading for the past few days had been what it had.[20]

Slowly and with strange majesty of purpose he rose to his feet. In that hubbub of confusion there was something about his deliberativeness and calm that gripped the chamber. The whole room became hushed and calm.

The chair recognized the Senator from Tennessee. Good old Andy Johnson! many of them must have thought. Here was a southern man. He'd mince no words in telling these northern fools of their folly. He wouldn't fail the land of his birth. Ever noted for their strange, magnetic qualities, Johnson's black eyes flashed about him and upward and around the now strangely quieted galleries.

The moment found him elated and strengthened by news that he could count on the leaders of eastern Tennessee for support. Only that morning, news had reached

him that a convention of leading citizens of his district
had met in convention a few days before and had passed
a resolution to the effect that secession was unthinkable
until every means for a compromise had been fairly and
honorably tried out.[21]

A copy of the resolution had been sent him with the
names of leading slaveholders affixed. He hoped for compromise, as a last hope.

Aware of his great task, Johnson didn't plunge into
his subject as many biographers would have us believe.
As we study that great speech today—a cold, logical document made lifeless by lack of his amazing delivery and
oratory—we realize he was first like an adroit fencer testing
out an antagonist. He was facing more than a single antagonist; he was facing a huge crowd whose passions had
soared above all powers of reason or logic. So he tricked
them to calm them.[22]

He urged the Senate to pass a resolution he had introduced five days before—an amendment to the Constitution
to prevent executive partiality resulting from majority
rule. He proposed a better balance in the White House
and on judicial benches. If the country had a northern
president it must elect a southern vice-president or
vice versa.

This was pleasant music to the malcontents, and he
continued to lull them with rebukes of northern unfairness
and highhandedness. But all the while he was working
towards his point with the cunningness of one able to use
words and arguments as a master musician utilizes notes.

But his next five words seemed like the judicial ulti-
matum of some demigod from on high. Like a mighty
broadside against the whole southern position:

"I am opposed to Secession. . . . If the doctrine of secession is to be carried out upon the mere whim of a state
this government is at an end! No state has a right to secede
from this Union without the consent of the other states
which ratified the compact!"

His listeners stiffened and came to life. Senators rose
angrily to their feet but he waved aside their interruptions

21

like a man impatient with flies. Their frenzied objections fell unheard against the new volume in his voice.

"The North is wrong in enacting so-called liberty bills in the teeth of the Constitution and the United States statutes. The South is equally wrong and now Florida, Louisiana and Texas, bought and paid for by all the states, are now endeavoring to back out of the contract!"

As he spoke, he not only stated facts and quoted authorities; he had the source material right there on his desk. More than once he cleverly inveigled other senators into reading laws and quotations for him so that none might accuse him of inaccuracy.

Once, Collamer, of Vermont, managed to gain the floor because Johnson had named his state as one of those which had violated the Constitution by having passed a so-called Liberty bill.

Again and again, members from the South, irate and vociferous, threw decorum to the winds in order to interrupt and heckle him. Johnson either ignored them or else laughed at them. The galleries, mostly southern cohorts, booed and hissed but Johnson's voice rose above the sounds in a mighty diapason[23]—at times to an awesome roar— again to the barest whisper which people struggled to hear. Some of his words had the sting of whiplashes; others cracked like rifle shots. Some sentences roared and reverberated, while others thundered.

"What is this issue?" Johnson scornfully cried. "It is this and only this, we are mad because Mr. Lincoln has been elected and we have not got our man. If we had got our man we should not be for breaking up the Union but as Mr. Lincoln IS elected, we are breaking up the Union. Am I to be so great a coward as to retreat from duty? No sirs! Here I will stand and meet the encroachments upon my country at the threshold!"[24]

Far into the next afternoon as well, arguing, berating, pleading, wheedling, scolding, challenging, and condemning those who sought to tear the Union assunder, he refused to be silenced. This was the battle of his life and the passionate words that flowed torrentially from his lips, and the irresistible logic pouring from his brain, were like the

22

high notes of a bugle, imperiously calling to a whole nation to follow on behind him.

Tired and lonely, Johnson came to the end. Fully aware and keenly conscious of his terrific responsibility for what he had said, Johnson nevertheless stalked proudly forth from the chamber, seemingly indifferent to the fact he had ventured his whole future and that of his country as well to the gamble of civil war.

Of applause there was none.[25] All the way out of the building and down the dusty, rutted avenue to his room in the Kirkwood Hotel, he was followed by a crowd of fuming, irate southerners who wished to fight with him. Even the lobby afforded no respite from their verbal onslaughts and insults. He wasn't afraid of them nor anybody else but he did want a little peace and he did want to tell Eliza about it all in a letter.[26] Once in his room, he poured out a long letter to her back in the peace and quiet of Greeneville, Tennessee.

That night his name and speech were on everyone's lips. Men crowded hotel lobbies and bars in the Capitol, heatedly to discuss the issues as he had outlined them. The cable and telegraph wires echoed his stirring plea from the Atlantic to the Pacific and from the Gulf to Canada. It was relayed around the world.

The effect on the Nation was astounding. It unified the North overnight. In the South it created consternation, but it stiffened their determination. It had thrown down the gauntlet for war.

For he had laid down a mighty principle. Wavering millions suddenly realized the Union was worth fighting and dying for. Johnson went to bed a tired man. He awakened to find himself the most discussed man in the whole Nation. Letters and telegrams poured in to him by the thousands. State legislators met to pass ardent resolutions of endorsement. The whole North seemed rising up like one man. The South was aghast and enraged; his effigy was burned countless times and the insulting messages and wires seemed without end. His office force found it impossible to answer the demand for copies of the speech, could not even answer promptly the innumerable invitations for him to come and make addresses here and there throughout the North.

When one examines the newspapers of that day, the brief comments accorded to a speech, which history has proved to be one of the most outstanding, are puzzling. But newspapers followed a peculiar style then. Stirring descriptions and overuse of adjectives were frowned upon. One finds only bare facts and one must draw his own conclusions.

The National Republican, of Washington, for December 20, 1860, for an example, covered the story like this: "Senator Johnson's speech was the topic of approbation at all the hotels last night. It was able and patriotic." No more and no less! Editorially, however, it also read: "New Yorkers of wealth ought to send a million copies of Andrew Johnson's speech to Southerners." Actually more than one-half million copies were printed. In other cities of the land, however, it was given greater praise and was more thoroughly analyzed.

Thus, his printed words lacked much that might reveal their great effect on a nation but there are plenty of comments left behind by his contemporaries and friends, and even enemies, to inform us how he affected people.

After that speech, life was never again the same for Andrew Johnson. Yesterday, as it were, he had been a plebian-nobody who had worked his way upward. Today his words and policy were even destined to strongly influence the president-elect—Abraham Lincoln—who was soon to succeed the confused and addled Buchanan.

CHAPTER 4

THE GATHERING STORM

To read tributes to a man, don't go to his friends. Turn rather to his enemies, for they are the ones who fully feel the weight of his powers. Alexander H. Stephens, to become vice-president of the Confederacy, amply proved this in the course of an interview with a newspaper reporter in 1875. But for Andrew Johnson, the South would have achieved her independence, Stephens thought. His speech of December 19, 1860, was "the most masterful effort delivered by man on earth."[27]

But in 1860 neither Stephens nor any other southern adherent had praise for the Tailor of Greeneville. His words still stung and burned. Southerners lost no opportunity to revile and castigate him inside and out of Congress. In fact they assailed him wherever they could get anyone to stop and listen. To them it was unthinkable that a southern Democrat, a North Carolinian by birth and a slaveholder himself, would turn on his "own people."

Most vituperative of all was Joe Lane, the Senator from Oregon, ex-southerner and former soldier in the Mexican War. In his campaign of villification and hate, he was enthusiastically supported by Wigfall, Benjamin, Tombs, and Iverson.[27]

Northern Congressmen, however, tried eagerly to become his friend. He was truly the "Man of the Hour" and from early morning to late at night he was surrounded by praising adherents. Newspapers all over the nation were making him a subject for constant conversation. His every word and thought seemed oracular.

Back in Tennessee, Johnson's speech had the effect of a bombshell, despite the assurance he had felt from the resolution insisting that every effort be made to compromise. A peculiar situation prevailed in the Volunteer State.[28]

The state was strongly Whig and there was a widespread belief that slavery and every other issue must compromise or give way to the preservation of the Union. Refusal to compromise, however, was quite another thing and the state's loyalty was subject to a number of factors.

In eastern Tennessee, rugged mountains necessitated small farms. The inhabitants were thrifty, religious, and highly industrious. Social conditions were such that a vigorous school of political thought was developed—a school that produced men of the Jackson-Johnson type. Slave labor had little place in the scheme of things. The people were too proud and independent. The few slaves in the district were largely used as domestic servants. Often they were treated as though they were members of the family, such as Johnson's servants.

Middle and western Tennessee, being largely rolling slopes and rich alluvial plains, brought about different conditions. Here were huge plantations where cotton and tobacco could be profitably raised on a large scale with slave labor. This system created great wealth for the few.

The state seethed in turmoil as tension mounted elsewhere. A border state, her sympathies were largely with the South. Governor Isham Harris was an out-and-out sympathizer with the Secessionists. He surrounded himself with similar others. The whole state became a turmoil. The legislature was called into secret session. Soon men were being whipped, shot, and hanged by one faction or another as sentiments became too openly expressed.[29]

Towards Johnson and his family, the Secessionists of Tennessee were extremely bitter. His mail overflowed with threats and vile abuse. His faithful friends and backers were alarmed. They wired and wrote him to exercise great care. Sure of himself, however, he went lustily on his tasks.

In Washington, the secession movement had caused turmoil. The local papers were filled with the brief statements of young southern belles returning to their homes from northern finishing schools. Not only the girls, but also the young males of northern colleges were leaving posthaste. *The National Republican,* for December 21, 1860, pictures the scene vividly. "Mr. Hammond, of South Carolina, absentee Congressman, sent for all his accumulated back-pay." Again: "Today Representative Miles, of South Carolina, told President Buchanan, 'If you send a solitary soldier to these parts, the instant the intelligence reaches our people—and we will take care that it does reach us before he reaches the forts—the forts will be taken because it is necessary for our safety and preservation.' "

Editorially the *Republican* then went on to say "And it was from this insolent menace that miserable old imbecile who occupies the post of Chief Magistrate of this great republic and Commander-in-Chief of its Army and Navy, basely succumbed and ignominiously shrunk from his duty."

Foreign powers were cautious. "The Austrian Consul at Charleston assured leading secessionists the Emperor of Austria would acknowledge the independence of South Carolina." When the Austrian *Charge d'Affaires* at Washington was questioned about this grave matter, he immediately replied: "His Majesty will hereafter try to get along without the consul's valued services."

No screaming headlines! No "blow-ups" to catch the eye and panic the mind. Just plain little paragraphs of solid type tucked here and there among funny patent medicine and other advertisements. Paragraphs, nevertheless, that men think and ponder.

President Buchanan, fine old man though he was, seemed not to realize his seeming lack of courage was hastening the strife. His very Cabinet, with the single exception of General Cass, openly sided with Secession. Several members should have been court-martialed and shot as traitors. They calmly had government gold and silver money shipped from northern and western sub-treasuries to others in the South where they could be swiftly seized—as they were— in the event of war.[30]

Thousands of muskets, rifles, revolvers, and other army equipment were shipped South from Rockford and other northern arsenals because of the traitorous acts of members of Buchanan's Cabinet. Because of the slavery issue involved, the timid Chief Executive might not have been able to have stopped the war but he could have made it a shorter one. Even as he equivocated what to do, southern agents were boldly and openly buying cannon, firearms, and ammunition in the North! And England was calmly shipping in vast supplies.[31]

January, 1861, found the Nation rumbling like a great volcano. There was no longer any hope for a compromise. Buchanan hesitated to act and both sides snarled and growled and waited for the other to commit some overt act.

Johnson, never timid or afraid in his life, took the bit in his teeth again on the 5th and 6th of February. With the applause and commendation of the whole North, he defended himself forcefully and masterly against Joe Lane, Judah Benjamin, and Jefferson Davis. It was another great speech and it rocked the Nation. Lincoln stood in the background and pondered deeply. He was trying to plan his policies and the Tailor was strongly influencing him.[32]

The avalanche toward war gained momentum. It might be stopped if the Administration were to act boldly before the South could fully arm and prepare itself. Johnson saw that it was necessary for him now to call spades by their name and that unless he further unified the North all hope for the Union was gone.

On March 2, he made another speech in the crowded Senate. Fearlessly he informed both Chair and crowded galleries that he stood among traitors who were even then urging that the flag be fired upon and our forts and arsenals seized. Challenged to name these traitors, he pointed to them with outstretched finger and blazing eyes and said you—and you—and you.[32]

Time and again, the Chair demanded the galleries be cleared of vociferous spectators. This time they were hur-rahing Andy Johnson! This time it seemed that every southern sympathizer was silent and frightened.

National newspapers gave greater prominence to this speech than the one of December 19 and 20.[33] Obviously, it was more to the point, more eloquently dramatic and undoubtedly marked the highest peak of popularity which he was to attain in life.

It is a strange thing to note that in referring to Jefferson Davis' willingness to "stab his mother country in the back" he quoted the soliloquy from Cardinal Wolsey—

28

Nay, then, farewell!
I have touched the highest point of all my greatness!
And from that full meridian of my glory
I haste now to my setting; I shall fall
Like a bright exhalation in the evening
And no man see me more!

War was close at hand. It was in the air—it was on everyone's lips.

Every effort at compromise failed. The peacemakers gave way to the trouble-makers. April 12, 1861, Fort Sumter was fired upon. Virginia had seceded and southern soldiers were streaming across the state toward the Capital. Confederate pickets were already on post at the very outskirts of Washington. Lincoln issued a proclamation for troops to defend the Nation.

The whole country stirred to action. Governor Harris, of Tennessee, refusing to wait on an election, boldly entered into a military pact with the newly established Confederate Government; called for a large army, levied new taxes and arrogantly wired Lincoln that his levy of men was to defend the state and not to help the Union. In the meanwhile, spring elections were on hand and not the least of the issues was the stand that Tennessee would take in the conflict.[34]

Johnson determined to return to his district and do his best to influence the people of his section to stand by the Union. It was an act that almost cost him his life more than a few times. At Lynchburg, Virginia, a highly inflamed mob surrounded the train. Savage cries of "Lynch the traitor!" came from every side. Several pushed their way into the coach and one pugnacious individual tried to pull Johnson's nose. Johnson fought him off.

Riding on the same train was Senator Wigfall, of Texas, and although they were enemies, Wigfall persuaded the crowd to let Johnson say a few words. Then he brought Johnson out on the platform, and he stunned the crowd into silence when he told them in ringing tones that he was a Union man and proud of it! Their imprecations and threats failed to daunt him.[35]

At Bristol, in his own district, a band of Confederates,

learning of his coming, hurried to the station, determined to lynch him. Around their failure to do so is an interesting story. A young Confederate officer, Captain A. G. Greenwood, appeared on the scene before the train came to a full stop as the roaring, infuriated crowd hurried forward, ordered the engineer to speed to Jonesboro before stopping!

"My orders came from President Jefferson Davis!" declared Greenwood in a statement issued after the war was over. "How President Davis learned of this mob I do not know but he telegraphed me orders to save Senator Johnson's life and I carried them out."[36]

Historians have often wondered whether or not this friendly action on the part of Davis was not in some way responsible for Johnson's clemency towards him when efforts were being made to try him for treason after the war had ended. It is something to speculate on, for there appears no data on the subject. While a prisoner in Fortress Monroe, Davis eulogized Johnson in no uncertain terms. However, there was always friction between them while they were in the Senate.

For more than a month, Johnson spoke day and night to gatherings in eastern Tennessee. Often, the meetings were turbulent and marked by fist fights. Frequently he spoke with a ready pistol beside him. Once, he was warned that if he spoke at a certain town one night he would be shot from the crowd. Johnson went there and spoke—holding his weapon in his hand and daring anyone to shoot him![37]

Knoxville, however, was about as far west as he could travel. Beyond that point, Governor Harris waited to place him under arrest. Had he been captured, his execution would have followed immediately, for tempers had been fanned to the flaming point. Already, unbelievable cruelties were being waged against Union men by roving bands. Many were hanged, beaten, tarred and feathered, and worse. Some were even hunted down by bloodhounds when they tried to escape from mobs.

It was a foregone conclusion that Secession would win out in the elections, but not so in East Tennessee. Thanks to Johnson's fervent appeals and those of a bevy of other men such as T. A. R. Nelson, "Parson" Brownlow, Horace Maynard, and Oliver P. Temple, the districts east of Knoxville showed a majority of almost twenty thousand voting to stay in the Union.[38]

From that moment on, pandemonium and terror broke loose. With the rest of the state in open rebellion, Governor Harris ordered General Felix K. Zollicoffer to subdue the section and what followed was sheer, brutal tragedy. While their wives and old men tried to carry on, the stalwarts either fled to join the Union armies or else took to the mountains and waged savage guerrilla warfare against their would-be conquerors. The First District, Johnson's home, gave more men to the Union Army than any congressional district in any of the other states.

Before Zollicoffer's troops arrived, however, the four eastern districts had done a most courageous thing. In the August elections, they pitted four Union men against the nominees chosen by the Governor to represent the state in the Southern Confederacy! They not only elected these four men in the face of sanguine odds, but they managed to seat two of them at Washington.

Of the four men thus elected, only Horace Maynard and George W. Bridges managed to escape the network closing in on the area. Bridges was captured by Confederate soldiers while making his way into Virginia with Thomas A. R. Nelson. Later, he managed to escape and reach Washington. Nelson, however, won freedom for himself only by signing a parole which forced him to remain inactive for the duration of the war.

With the Governor and the rest of the state in a frenzy at what they called the traitorous acts of the Loyal Unionists, Zollicoffer and his men showed no mercy. They rode roughshod over the whole countryside. They stripped it of crops and livestock and what they didn't use themselves was shipped to the Confederacy. Nor were their depredations all. Roving bands, bushwhackers and guerrillas utilized the times for self-gain and sadist sports. They hanged men, raped women, burned, stole, tortured. Prisons and hospitals bulged and groaned with human misery.[39]

High among the crags of the Smokies or else hidden in

the secret, wooded coves, the Loyal Unionists led hunted, haunted lives. Food was hard to get. Misery and death were their common lot but still they held on. For good Ol' Andy Johnson had gone safely to Washington and he had promised to send Federal troops, money, and guns.

Johnson was a marked man, often escaping capture and certain death by bare minutes, thanks to timely warnings. On June 14, 1861, he managed to escape into Kentucky and from there made his way back to Washington. His family had to be left behind and Johnson was not to see them again until after the war had ended, even though he was destined to return soon to Tennessee as Military Governor of the state. As such, his headquarters at Nashville were hundreds of miles from the old home town and most of those miles were filled with formidable southern armies who defied all efforts to drive them out of the district.[40]

Despite his high position, Johnson found it almost impossible to communicate with his beloved family and the few letters to his wife which he managed to have smuggled in are tragic in their pent-up longings.[40]

The events of the war and Johnson's energetic part in them made him more obnoxious than ever to the enemy. Finally, as retaliation against him, General Zollicoffer confiscated his property and ordered Mrs. Johnson and the children to leave instantly under penalty of military arrest. Already invalided by consumption and having only been permitted to eat through the generosity of former slaves, Eliza painfully made her way North with the children. Her trip en route was a hideous experience we would prefer to say nothing about.[41]

As the war unfolded and the tragic months went by, Grant and his armies rolled down into central and western Tennessee. But Andy Johnson's beloved section remained firmly held by the Confederates who deemed it too valuable to relinquish. It was too rich in salt, coal, iron, saltpetre, and all-important bacon and beef.

Returning to Washington, Johnson was working day and night to promote swift assistance for his people. President Lincoln studied him long and hard, finally talking him into resigning as a Senator and then appointing him Military Governor of Tennessee, with the rank of brigadier general. Headquarters were to be at Nashville where northern forces were still holding firm, despite great pressure.

It was a more important step and his actions as Governor would quickly endear him to the whole North.

CHAPTER 5

LINCOLN'S CHOICE

Laura Carter, pretty little spitfire of twenty years, was in trouble. Union officers objected to her spitting down upon them from the steps of her father's hotel, The St. Cloud, in Nashville. So, they arrested her.

"Governor, I hated to make this arrest on account of you and her father," explained General Ebenezer Dumont to the new Military Governor of Tennessee. "But she has been indulging in all forms of contempt and I thought it about time to check her. When I told her that she ought to behave herself while you were a guest at her father's hotel, she defied you and said she would yet dance on your grave!"

Andrew Johnson raised his head from the pile of papers he was studying and grinned good-naturedly at the irate commander of Nashville's defending forces. With rare insight into the not too-distant future, he said something Ben Truman, his secretary, was to remember:

"Oh, you musn't mind these little rebels, General. There is no harm in Laura. Dance on my grave, will she? She will plant flowers instead! I'll take care of her. Let her go!"[42]

Laura Carter wasn't the only Tennessean who wanted to spit on Andrew Johnson in 1862 when he returned to Nashville as Lincoln's Military Governor. Literally thousands would gladly shoot or hang him and many were the plans for his kidnapping or assassination that were thwarted by vigilant friends or the soldiery. In fact, the whole fury and spleen of the state's secessionists seemed to rain down on his head.

It seemed bad enough that his speeches had been a factor in northern solidarity, but it passed belief that Lincoln would use him to drag or beat them back into the Federal fold. Was there ever such a vile wretch? Such a black traitor to his state? Assassination was too good for such a dog!

In 1861, Senator Johnson had escaped from East Tennessee by the very skin of his teeth. On June 14, he passed through Cumberland Gap, headed for Kentucky, with rebel soldiers hard on his heels. Their orders, issued from Nashville, had been to shoot him summarily as a traitor. Highly placed old friends at the Capitol risked their own lives to warn him and even his erstwhile enemy, "Parson" Brownlow, urged him to escape while it was still possible.

In Washington, Johnson had plunged into the task of trying to succor his hard-pressed district. They needed money, supplies, and guns, and he neglected no opportunity to plead their cause. On July 26, he had offered a resolution in the Senate that is worth recalling. It had encountered the causes and purposes of the war, contending the North had no purpose of oppression, conquest, or subjugation. Rather, the sole thought was "to defend the Constitution and to maintain its supremacy and to preserve the Union with all the dignity, equality and rights of the several states unimpaired and as soon as these objects are accomplished, the war ought to cease."

The measure passed the Senate by a vote of thirty-five to five. In the House, a similar motion was introduced by Crittenden. Notably, Thaddeus Stevens refused to vote on the resolution in the House and Charles Sumner did likewise in the Senate. Already these were spinning their web against the days of hate and revenge.[43]

Now stateless, because all of Tennessee, save his section, had gone over to the Confederacy, Johnson spent much time trying to reach the ears of high Union officers. He wanted help for his people and he wanted it in a hurry. There were many loyal citizens in eastern Tennessee and their plight was tragic. Johnson fumed and fretted and even raised private funds from wealthy northern sympathizers.[44] Meanwhile, General Grant was getting things done instead of engaging in petty headquarters' wars. He moved his army down into middle Tennessee and captured Forts Henry and Donelson. The Confederates had to evacuate Nashville in late February, 1862, and their retreat took them almost to the Virginia and North Carolina lines.

35

This was Lincoln's chance and the very first tactical gain of the war. He now saw the opportunity of re-establishing state government in Tennessee. He had sent for Andrew Johnson. Would he be willing to resign from the Senate and return to Nashville as Military Governor?

Lincoln received his answer. By March 12, Johnson was back in the state capitol, in the very middle of danger. Bragg's army was forty miles away at Murfreesboro, threatening to strike at any moment. Governor Harris, fleeing for safety before Grant, re-established his Confederate state government at Memphis. The bulk of Nashville's population was Confederate to the core.

One of Johnson's first acts was a proclamation to the people guaranteeing one and all the protection of the government, provided they would take an oath of allegiance to the United States. Amnesty and pardon were offered to all save the "conscious leaders in treason."[45]

Considering the precarious situation of those to whom the proclamation was addressed, it was a compassionate, generous offer. The North, printing copies, approved with gusto, but not so the rebel populace. From pulpit, press, and street, the people were urged to resist. Only a few came forward to take the oath. Among these were two former governors of the state—William Campbell and Neill S. Brown.[46]

Johnson promptly suspended the *Nashville Times* for its belligerent statements. The officials of the city government refused to come forward and take the oath, and he threw them out of office and replaced them with loyal Union men. Six ministers preached traitorous sermons to their flocks and Andy clapped them into jail and imprisoned a judge.[47]

Such stern moves helped, but they were not enough. The town was filled with refugees and many were the wives and families of Confederate soldiers. Johnson, at his wit's end to feed and clothe them, solved the matter by assessing all wealthy secessionists for their support. An eye for an eye, whenever he heard of maltreatment of unionists in other parts of the state, he took hostages and shipped them at their own expense into the deep South.

Back in Washington that June, his famous Homestead

Bill was passed and made a law. But Johnson had no time now to celebrate even such good news. Day and night, he was kept busy with the thousand and one problems of suppressing rebellion and restoring civil government.

Slowly the days and weeks went by and every hour of them was a harrowing strain upon the Tailor of Greeneville. His face became deeply lined and his temper, never too stable, became choleric.

On either side of him, and not many miles away, were impressive southern armies under efficient leaders. From the safety of their ranks, the two famous cavalry raiders, Morgan and Forrest, made slashing, terrorizing sallies where they were least expected, leaving a trail of death and desolation in their wake.

Ranking as a brigadier general in the army in addition to his Military Governorship, Johnson had other troubles besides his constantly mounting civil ones. He was forever clashing with the commanders of the Union armies because he insisted they drive the Confederates out of eastern Tennessee. His quarrels with Buell became epic and even Lincoln was drawn into them, ever taking Johnson's side, because, like Johnson, he realized the strategic value of the loyal region, reaching like a spearhead into the very vitals of the Confederacy. Johnson wanted to restore democratic government in Tennessee.

For the Unionists of Tennessee, he needed victory badly. Charged with the task was Don Carlos Buell, stubborn, high-handed, and haughty, with little patience for politicians. To Buell, Johnson was a meddling civilian. Had Buell been enabled to win, the inevitable clash in personality with the intemperate Governor might not have been so bad. But in his campaign, Buell was slow to follow up advantages and finally was soundly baffled and thrashed at Perryville, and the campaign to conquer East Tennessee collapsed.

Johnson was intractable. He would not, could not, accept defeat and, with mounting fury, he pled with Lincoln and Stanton to remove Buell. He accused him not only of incompetence but even of disloyalty. Buell's failure led to Johnson's success. Lincoln, whose confidence in Johnson was growing daily, replaced Buell with Rosecrans. On November 18, 1862,

Johnson wrote to Lincoln: "I feel in strong hopes that things will go well in a few days as we have a man at the head of the army who will fight. I sometime ago advised you that Buell would never redeem East Tennessee, and stated substantially what he has since proved himself to be."[48]

Tennessee had literally become the leading battlefield of the war. A total of seven hundred engagements was fought on her soil and of these several were battles of major importance. There was Shiloh, where the great rebel leader, Albert Sidney Johnston, was killed. There was the gory Chickamauga; Snodgrass Hill and the pond at its foot that became actually red with the blood of struggling soldiers; Franklin, where eleven generals were killed or wounded; Chattanooga and the "Battle above the Clouds"; and Murfreesboro saddening the nation with its ghastly toll.

In October, Johnson's family managed to reach him. His Greeneville properties had all been seized by the Confederacy and sold at public auction. His family had been ordered out of town and granted passes to the Kentucky line. By now his wife was in the first stages of her fatal illness and so, too, was Andrew, Jr., his eight-year-old son. Both Charles and Robert, his older sons, were cavalry officers in Tennessee regiments. Now and then, they managed to slip into Nashville for brief family reunions.

For a few months that fall, Johnson stumped what portions of the state he could reach, trying to weld the people back into the Union, as guerrilla bands waited to ambush him. Others tore up the rails ahead of his trains. Often he escaped death by what may well be called miracles.[49]

Lincoln himself saw to it that he was amply surrounded by bodyguards. Lincoln was beginning to have more than a little respect for this doughty southern democrat. He had men detailed from Ohio, Michigan, and Minnesota regiments, and they entered their tasks with a will, for Johnson was a man's man — fearless, ever ready to fight; and when he had a speech to make, it was always something the men wanted to hear.

On one of these visits away from his new home, Johnson penned a tragic, badly misspelled letter to Eliza.

I feel sometimes like giving up in despare; but this will not do. We must hold out to the end, this rebellion is wrong and must

38

be put down let cost what it may in life and treasure. I intend to appropriate the remainder of my life to the redemption of my adopted home, East Tennessee and you and Mary must not be weary, it is our fate and we should be willing to bear it cheerfully. Impatience and dissatisfaction will not better it or shorten the time of our suffering.[50]

That summer, General Bragg invaded Kentucky and almost all the Union troops were hurried back after him. Morgan, the Raider, seized the chance to make swift, savage forays into Kentucky and Missouri. Then, joining with Forrest, he besieged Nashville. From September 15 to November 14, the city was cut off from the outside world.

For weeks, the environs of the city were under shot and shell. The Capitol was fortified and barricaded. Johnson and his little staff slept with their clothes on, watching the progress of the fighting from convenient windows. Three times during that harrowing siege, Union generals decided to evacuate the city. They felt it was impossible to hold Tennessee, let alone conquer it.

But Andrew Johnson was adamant. Abandon Tennessee? Over his dead body! "I'm no military man!" he thundered from his office, "but everyone who talks of surrender I will shoot!" Even Lincoln had to laugh later on when the story was told him about how Johnson prayed for victory.[51]

It seemed that during the siege, Granville Moody, a famous Methodist evangelist and Abolitionist orator, came to Johnson to inquire how things were going. He found Johnson in a rage. "Going! Why, Moody, we've been sold out! Buell is a traitor. He's going to evacuate the city and in twenty-four hours we'll all be in the hands of the rebels! Can you pray? Do so then!"

Moody dropped to his knees and began an old-fashioned prayer for courage and victory. Johnson kept interrupting him with fervent "Amens!" in typical Methodist style. Moody's prayer grew more fervent and the Governor crawled to his side and flung his arms around him in an excess of emotion. Both cried out a final loud "Amen!" and then rose up and faced each other.

"Moody," apologized the Governor, "don't think I'm a religious man because of this. I am not and never pretended

39

to be. But there is one thing about it — I believe in God Almighty and in truth and I'll be damned if Nashville shall be surrendered!"[52]

Nor was it. On September 14, the Confederates were led forward by a ruse and so badly beaten and routed that they fled. But their departure to older lines only added to the Governor's tasks and problems.

January, 1863, saw personal tragedy for him. Dr. Charles Johnson, their first-born son, was thrown from his horse and killed. Eliza, now an invalid confined to bed, never recovered from the shock.

With the arrival of General Rosecrans during the fall before, to help relieve Nashville, military matters went better in the state. However, there were the bloody battles of Lookout Mountain and Missionary Ridge to be fought ere the Confederates were sent reeling back.

Johnson overlooked no opportunity during the months of re-establishing civil order and government. Lincoln and even Stanton were full of praise and ever ready to help. There is a letter to Johnson from Secretary Stanton which today almost surpasses belief when one realizes what was to transpire later between the two men.

> This department called you from the comparatively safe and easy duties of civil life, to place you in front of the enemy. In a position of personal toil and danger, perhaps more hazardous than was encountered by any other citizen or military officer of the United States, you have maintained yourself. Through unparalleled trials you have gallantly periled all that was dear to man on earth. Your services have been patriotic and able, you have been worthy of the confidence of the government, and the thanks of the department are extended to you.[53]

Sometime earlier than this, Lincoln was having a long chat with Speaker Colfax of the House of Representatives. Colfax put down what Lincoln said that day about Johnson: "Andrew has never embarrassed me to the slightest degree." This puts the lie to Charnwood who wrote that Lincoln could never bear the sight of Johnson.[54]

Besides the military battles then being fought over Tennessee there were political ones. Lincoln wanted the state returned to the Union but it would require a majority vote.

40

Johnson bent his every hour to the task. By late summer, 1863, as the tides of war seethed back and forth, the Union Party split up and Radicals and Conservatives faced each other with passion in their hearts. Behind Johnson's back, men constantly sought to knife him by personal appeals to Lincoln for his highhandedness. Lincoln would only smile and tell them to go back and make peace with him.[55]

Lincoln urged Johnson to employ Negro troops, the supply of manpower being low. Although Johnson had contemplated their use, he nonetheless was hesitant for fear of injuring unionist sentiment. Finally, however, the details were worked out. Slaves of loyalists were used and Johnson's idea that the owners be given a bounty of $300 and the slave to receive any other pay, including payment for substituting, was accepted by the President. The recruitment of Negro troops was met with much success.[56]

The President had reiterated that the war was fought for the preservation of the Union, nonetheless emancipation was continually pressed upon him. He entertained ideas of compensated emancipation but the border states reacted negatively. Finally on January 1, 1863, was issued the Emancipation Proclamation, freeing the slaves in enemy territory, which was no freedom at all.

The proclamation posed a special problem for Johnson and Tennessee, a great part of which was still in Confederate hands. Johnson had, like Lincoln, held that this was a crusade to save the Union. But he was moving toward ideas of freeing the slaves. "I am for the government above all earthly possessions, if it perish, I do not want to survive it. I am for it, though slavery should be struck from existence . . . if you persist in forcing the issue of slavery against the government, I say in the face of Heaven, give me my government and let the Negro go." His hatred of aristocracy upon which the peculiar institution was based also made the road to emancipation less rocky for him. I am not for "a slave aristocracy," he had declared.

There were, however, practical considerations. Johnson was forced to move slowly for fear of losing what Unionists he had. Using his great influence with Lincoln, he had the state exempted. He wrote, "Your proclamation of the 1st, excepting

41

Tennessee, has disappointed and disarmed many who were complaining and denouncing it as unjust and unwise. I think the exception in favor of Tennessee will be worth much to us, especially when we can get to discuss it before the people."

Slaves were freed but not until the amendments to the Constitution were ratified in 1865, and then under Governor Brownlow the state moved slowly toward the Freedman's political rights. James G. Blaine in his *Twenty Years* asserts that both Lincoln and Johnson at a later date came to regard the exemption as a mistake, but many years later a scholar of the period concluded that "the considerate treatment of Tennessee by the President on the slavery issue clearly helped the Union cause."[57] Such a policy was Johnson's, however.

There isn't space here, nor is it our purpose to chronicle the bloody, drawn-out events of the Civil War and what took place in the Volunteer State. Johnson, in his zeal for his own loyal and suffering district, performed unflinchingly to remove the Confederate armies. Not until the fall of 1864, was General Rosecrans able to retake Knoxville and liberate the thousands of Unionists and reunite them with their families. The scenes that were enacted the day of his entry would touch even the stoniest-hearted. Literally by the thousands, mountain people—men, women, children, sons, daughters, fathers, and mothers—were reunited after four tragic years of suffering. Down from the peaks, hills, and coves of the Smokies they poured to welcome or to try and find their kinsmen.[58]

September of that year brought the news that the Andrew Johnson guard, composed of former townspeople who had gone to Nashville to serve him, had suddenly raided Greeneville during the early dawn and had shot and killed General John H. Morgan, the Raider, as he struggled to flee. The news was so cheering, in view of Morgan's terrible career, that it was hurried to Lincoln's desk by the War Department the moment received.

In 1864, National election time was rolling around again and soon there would be a mighty convention held in Baltimore for the purpose of naming a ticket. Lincoln had his ideas on the subject. He wanted re-election, for the war was far from over.

Shortly after the battle of Resaca, Ben C. Truman, an old Johnson lieutenant and member of his staff in Nashville, returned from Georgia to the state capitol. On the street he encountered a former newspaper friend with whom he held a brief reunion.

"What brings you down here?" he questioned, the amenities once over. His newspaper friend made a great show of secrecy. "I am here a volunteer aid on General Sickles' staff. The President has sent him here on an important mission—can't you guess it?" ". . . He has come down here to look after Johnson" . . . "to see what he is doing. To look into his habits. The President wants Johnson on the ticket with him. . . ."

It was about eleven o'clock and the tired Military Governor had long since gone to bed. But Truman knew this was tremendous news, and he had immediately awakened Johnson and poured out what he had just learned. Johnson sat upright. His words came crisp and fast: "Truman! I want you to leave for Washington tomorrow. Go direct to Colonel Forney . . . ask him to look after my interests."

CHAPTER 6

FATE SHOWS HER PATTERN

Eighteen sixty-four was a most crucial year in Lincoln's life. His hold on the people seemed to be slipping, and deep in his heart he did not think he stood a chance of re-election. The high honor of the place meant nothing to him. He wanted to see the war finished and the Nation well on the way to reconstruction ere he stepped down and handed over the reins to another.

The North was war weary and heart torn.[59] It was sick of mounting casualty lists and an ever-growing taxation which seemed impossible to meet. Business firms were failing all over the land, and victory seemed farther away than ever.

Infinitely worse, there was fear that England and France might yet recognize the Confederate States and openly furnish aid. Already the South had received considerable support from England and there had been many who urged we declare war on England for these acts. Nothing would have suited some British statesmen more than to see the United States split up and weakened.

As early as August 23, 1864, Lincoln felt his administration was almost over. On that day he wrote a memo to that effect in which he offered to be of every help to his successor— regardless of whom he might be. Without disclosing the contents of the memorandum, he had each member of the Cabinet sign his name to the back after noting the date. Months later, he showed them what he had written!

It was obvious to Lincoln that much of the support he needed would have to come from the Democrats of the country. A "war Democrat" as vice-president would give the appearance of National rather than sectional unity to the Party. The Republican Party was slowly but surely splitting up, and new blood was vital if it were to be preserved. Already many of its leaders were becoming known as Radicals because of their viewpoint on the Negro question. It was their expressed theory that the Negro was ready for all the rights of citizenship. Obviously, their plan was to win over this new colored vote.

Vice-President Hamlin, the incumbent, was a Democrat but too little known throughout the Nation to have much weight or power at the ballot box. Obviously, a new vice-presidential candidate was needed, and it was to be desired that he have a following in the South where Reconstruction of a sort was already under way.

For a while, Lincoln pondered over the selection of General Ben Butler. He even went so far as to discuss this with his advisors and then had Butler sounded out on the vice-presidential slate even though he personally despised the man and had once said of him, "He is as full of poison gas as a dead dog."[60] But Lincoln was man enough to hold the welfare of his country high above personal feelings.

Simon Cameron and William H. Armstrong, both outstanding Republican leaders from Pennsylvania, were sent to Butler's headquarters to see how Butler felt on the matter. What Butler told them was astounding.

The Beast of New Orleans, as southern women dubbed him, bluntly declined the honor. "I prefer to stay in the army. There is nothing in the vice presidency. Tell Mr. Lincoln . . . I would not quit the field to be vice president, even with himself as president unless he will give me bond with sureties, in full sum of his four years salary, that he will resign within three months after his inauguration!"[61]

Butler had long cherished hopes of becoming president himself. A movement had been under way for some time for his nomination to the post and his refusal to entertain running for vice-president on the ticket with Lincoln is somewhat understandable.

Lincoln knew, of course, what Butler's ambitions were, and it is quite possible that he was attempting to nullify him as a presidential rival. Whatever his reason, posterity can rejoice that nothing came of the effort. Worthless as a soldier and of dubious value as a legislator, Butler can now be regarded as one of those strange monstrosities who develop and come to the fore in time of crisis.

Already the terrible forces were shaping up around and about Lincoln which were to cost the country dearly. Weary of war and unable to see a quick victory, the people at large were more than willing to listen to those who preached that a change of administration was the one thing needed to ensure peace.

The political record of the year 1864 was a strange hodgepodge of plot and counterplot — of little groups trying to groom their own candidate with whom they meant to replace Lincoln. Lincoln's own Cabinet members were up to their necks in this labyrinth of plotting and whispers. Pulling this string and that, were such malcontents as William Lloyd Garrison and that be-whiskered busybody of all busybodies, Horace Greeley.

But Lincoln was no fool and it is not without reason that he has been dubbed "The Master Politician of the Ages." He had friends and not all his Cabinet were unfaithful. Seward and Blair were competent and knew their mass psychology. Outside of the Cabinet he had as allies such powerful figures as Simon Cameron, A. K. McClure, Thrulow Weed, Henry J. Raymond, and more than a few others.

At first the Radicals pinned their hopes on General Butler. Some of them felt if only he could encompass and execute a great Union victory in Virginia that the Nation would ring with his praises and nomination would be easy. They were cold-blooded about this; they made secret plans for Butler to carry out a battle independent of approval from the War Department! Adam Gurowski offers some of the detail in his remarkable diary under date of January 30, 1864.[62]

In a letter to Butler, he urges him to lead a secret expedition from Fortress Monroe against Richmond. He warns him not to tell anyone about his plans. When the "hour comes, strike the blow without letting out your secret. Report to the rulers —not Lincoln—when half way before Richmond." A great action, a bold action, and Lincoln's chances vanish as a nightmare.

With only his personal ambitions directing him, Butler threw his trusting men forward into an impossible scheme

46

for glory. It proved a hideous failure and two hundred of his men sacrificed their lives to his ambitions. The War Department was furious. Butler evaded much censure by reporting to President Lincoln that a traitorous New York soldier had disclosed his plans to the enemy and, but for Lincoln's orders suspending capital punishment in the army, we would have hanged him. Butler's men might have hanged HIM instead, had they but known how they had been used.

From Butler, the Radicals turned to Lincoln's Secretary of the Treasury, Salmon Chase. For months, this two-faced traitor ran his course until Lincoln cornered and exposed him.

Chase's sudden withdrawal was another body blow at the plans of the Radicals. Charles Sumner, Thad Stevens, Ben Wade, and the others were at the end of their string and about ready to cry quits. But other elements among the Republican Party were still hopeful. These were chiefly Abolitionists and the Missouri Radical Republicans, led by General John C. Fremont. Boldly they took the bit in their own teeth and called a National Republican Convention to assemble in Cleveland the last of May.[63]

Little resulted from this assembly and the efforts of some four hundred men whom the people thought of as "crackpots" ended in failure. Their use of the phrase National Republican Convention, however, gave Lincoln a splendid idea. He determined a new party would tender him the nomination for a second term and in his study was promptly born the new National Union Party. Calls to assemble in Baltimore, June 7 and 8, were hurriedly sent out.[64]

For many years a controversy raged over the question of whether or not Lincoln had asked that Johnson be selected as his running mate.

The argument chiefly arose over the fact that Lincoln confided in few men and those men were as secretive as himself. Time seems to have proved, however, that just before the convention assembled Lincoln had made known his choice to at least three of his political lieutenants, namely, Simon Cameron, Alexander K. McClure, and S. Newton Pettis, all from Pennsylvania. He not only told them his choice but he asked them to handle the matter for him as secretly as possible. They did so with surprising adroitness and many were the political apple carts they upset during those two hot June days.

Lincoln's final choice of Johnson was no mystery. His obstinate courage, his love for the Union and the tremendous sacrifices he had already made for it had long aroused Lincoln's admiration. The two men had known each other for many years, starting in the House of Representatives; until now they had never been close friends. In fact, they had constantly fought each other politically, and when Lincoln first ran for the presidency, Johnson did his best to defeat him.

When Lincoln sent General Sickles to Nashville to check on Johnson's suitability for the post of vice-president, it was largely to ascertain his executive abilities. If, as Military Governor, Johnson had been cruel or tyrannical, he would have not been suitable at all. General Sickles' report has never been uncovered by any historian, as far as we can determine, but it is obvious that it was satisfactory to Lincoln.

At the Baltimore Convention of the newly formed Union Party, as a courtesy to Hamlin, the first ballot was given him. His own lieutenants felt sure of his success but the adroit maneuvering of Cameron, McClure, and Pettis proved too much for them; the result, Johnson 200, Dickenson 113, Hamlin 145, and Butler 26. Dickenson was counted out when Johnson was the choice of Dickenson's New York Delegation.[65] Johnson finally won the unanimous ballot and his name went before the Nation as Lincoln's running mate.[65]

Much of the controversy that arose over Lincoln's final choice of Johnson was caused by John Nicolay.[66] Nicolay was an unofficial visitor to the convention, and although he was perhaps invited to write his impressions back to the White House, was in no sense a personal representative of Lincoln, as he led many people to believe. Vainly he had tried to ascertain Lincoln's choice for the vice-presidency but Lincoln was too smart for him. He assured Nicolay he wanted things left to delegates.[67]

Years later, in 1891, when Hamlin died, Nicolay made public a telegram he had sent to his widow. In that telegram he assured her that one of Lincoln's regrets had been that the Baltimore Convention had failed to follow his advice and renominate her late husband.

Alexander McClure, then editor of a Philadelphia newspaper, promptly denied Nicolay's statement and in an editorial, which was quoted all over the country, gave his side of the story. Nicolay took issue with McClure and in the resultant controversy went down in defeat and humiliation when McClure assured readers he didn't know what he was talking about; he had been but an humble clerk and never a confidant of the Great Emancipator. Simon Cameron and Colonel Pettis supported McClure in his contentions and Nicolay retreated.[68]

The Nation took the news of Johnson's nomination with mixed emotion—praise, humor, and sneers. Thaddeus Stevens asked with great heat: "Can't the Republican Party find someone for vice-president without going into a damned little Rebel territory to pick him out?" *The New York World* sneered and called the ticket one composed of "Gawks, rail-splitters and tailors." But many others took a sensible view and declared it would balance the Republican Party and give it new vitality.[69]

The political cartoons of that day prodded the candidates with their subtlety and humor. One newspaper remarked: "They have a railsplitter and a buffoon for the head of the ticket, and upon the tail they have a boorish tailor."[70]

In Chicago, a little later, the Democrats held their own national convention and, despite strenuous efforts to oppose him, General McClellan was nominated on the first ballot. It is interesting to note that the Democratic platform contended the war was a failure and that immediate efforts be made to bring about peace.

Busy fighting the war, the whole country now found itself fighting another one of politics. The situation was grave. It seems of striking interest to quote here a letter from *The*

Age of Hate, by George Fort Milton. It was written by Nathanial P. Sawyer, of Pittsburgh, to Andrew Johnson:[71]

> Oh, how I wish it had been you for the presidency! Then the Union party would not have been divided. Freemont would have supported you and we could have taken you to the White House without trouble. I am sorry, very sorry, that you have not been associated with a better man than Lincoln. But He that doeth all things well, have no doubt, will control this matter, and should Lincoln be successful, may He in His own good time make Andrew Johnson President and restore our unfortunate country once more to peace and happiness.

Down in Tennessee, the Tailor had his hands full. He had civil government to maintain; he had to prepare Tennessee for a return to the Union and he must carry the state for the Union party. It was no light load. Guerrillas were still sweeping over the First and Second Districts and the state at large was not responding well to the emancipation program. Drastic tests and oaths were requisite for voters ere success could be assured at election time.

Johnson had to resort to some adroit maneuvering for success at the polls.[72] The test oath he and his friends finally devised practically shut out any and all chances for McClellan's election. McClellan's friends were so chagrined they went to Washington, but Lincoln gave them little sympathy. He was fighting a battle for the Union, and he was short and to the point. He told them it was up to Johnson, and that they would do well to follow him.

From all over the country came urgent requests that Johnson come here or there to make speeches. His time was at a premium, but somehow he managed to make a few hurried trips to Ohio and Indiana where he addressed great crowds and was enthusiastically received. People flocked to hear this militant man who arraigned and damned the aristocrats in unforgettable sentences. His argument against McClellan was effective and simple: Such a president as McClellan would permanently establish slavery and forever degrade common labor!

Johnson's test-oath scheme insured Lincoln's election and his own, in Tennessee. Guerrilla warfare prevented many a middle and west Tennessee polling place to be open, but when the returns finally came in the Union Party carried the state by well over twenty-five thousand. Their victory throughout the Nation was equally impressive. Of twenty-two states whose votes Congress recognized, the Party carried all but three. Out of a total vote of 4,115,902, it won by about three hundred thousand.[73]

Again Abraham Lincoln was the choice of the people as their leader and to help him now there was a fighting man. The Radicals were spoiling for a fight. One of their first acts was to throw out the votes of Tennessee in protest against Lincoln's reconstruction plans. The state of Louisiana, having carried out Lincoln's wishes in regard to a test oath, duly went to the polls and elected a new and loyal government. They sent Senators and Representatives to Washington. There the Radicals, led by Charles Sumner, Thad Stevens, *et al,* defeated Lincoln's plans by withholding recognition. It was the dawn of trouble for the South.

In Nashville on the night of November 4, there was wild rejoicing over the election of Andrew Johnson. He made a stirring speech against a background of waving torches which cast weird reflections on a sea of excited black and white faces.

What he said doesn't matter very much. What mattered, however, were the words of his speech on June 9, 1864, when he accepted the nomination for vice-president: "I am opposed to treating secessionists as anything but rebels," he had vehemently cried to a stunned crowd. "They have forfeited for the time being the right to vote and hold office. They should be compelled to submit to a severe ordeal before restoration to citizenship. Their property should be forfeited and divided among the slaves!"

The Radicals had accepted this speech at its face value.[74] Here was a man, they felt, who would go along with them in their plans to fatten themselves on the stricken South. As for the aristocrats of the South, they could only tremble and wait for the worst.

The inauguration was sensational. Johnson made the sorriest blunder of his career, one that he and the country were to pay for dearly and one which continues to besmirch his memory. The Vice-President, bellowing out his address to amazed and shocked listeners, was drunk.

It is difficult to get at the truth in view of the gossipy tales, stories by jaundiced-eyed enemies and the lack, from consternation, of good newspaper reporting. There seem to be mitigating circumstances. Johnson had been ill from an attack of typhoid fever. For this reason, he tried to avoid the inauguration, but he attended at Lincoln's insistence. On the way he spoke at Ohio but owing to the state of his health he was forced to discontinue. Upon his arrival in Washington, March 3, he took to his bed at Kirkwood House where a physician prescribed stimulants. That evening, Colonel Forney and a party of celebrators came to his room. They were very much in their cups, but Johnson seems not to have imbibed.

The following day Johnson took two drinks on an empty stomach. He entered a packed, overheated chamber, took the oath and gave a badly prepared, incoherent speech.

Lincoln, with Johnson's friends, perceived something amiss. After the ceremony, he was taken to the home of Francis Preston Blair where he recuperated under a doctor's care.

Several days later, Hugh McCulloch approached Lincoln on the unfortunate events of March 4; he answered seriously:

> I have known Andy Johnson for many years; he made a bad slip the other day, but you need not be scared; Andy ain't a drunkard.

The mischief, however, had now been done and the whole Nation soon knew about the drunken vice-president. Johnson kept himself abed for a while. He should have stayed back in Tennessee until he had recovered entirely from his fever. His doctor issued a statement or two which didn't help matters. Charles Sumner and others kept the issue alive in the Congress. The Radicals passed several regulations about the use of intoxicants in the building and went on record to deny membership on any committee to a congressman for his "habitual use of intoxicants," as the Radicals continued their own use of spirits.[75]

CHAPTER 7

APRIL 14

In the early evening of April 14, Washington was a bustling, happy town. The news of the surrender of Lee to Grant was now a matter of history, and word of the capitulation of other Confederate generals was expected momentarily. The glittering social life of the city, rapidly being released from the gloom of war and lists of casualties, was beginning to bloom again. Not the least sign of this new relaxation was that President Lincoln and his lady were attending a comedy starring the vivacious Laura Keene, whose presence in the cast, it was hoped, would brighten an otherwise dull piece.

Governor Leonard J. Farwell, a friend of Johnson, attended the performance at Ford's theater. The Vice-President remained at his hotel, the Kirkwood. Farwell laughed with the audience as the play spun on. Suddenly frivolity died. Farwell heard, as though in a nightmare, the pistol shot that rocked the earth. He saw Booth stagger across the stage, heard his terrible cry about traitors. A quick-witted man, he instantly realized what had happened. His one thought was that Johnson was now President and must be guarded at all costs. The horrible thought even flashed through his mind that perhaps he was already too late!

Without waiting at the theater for any definite news, he sped off for the Kirkwood House. Panting and almost incoherent, he plunged into the lobby and threw pandemonium over the loiterers. Spencer, one of the clerks, hurried to him. "Guard the door!" cried the ex-Governor. "Guard Johnson's room! The President has been assassinated!" To another clerk, too startled to speak, he made the same demand. "Guard the door! President Lincoln has been murdered!"

Spent and weak-kneed from his exertion and the terrible strain, he clawed his way to Room 68, where he had left Johnson. Again and again, he banged on the door. At the top

53

of his voice, he cried out, "Governor Johnson! If you are in the room, I must see you at once!"

His words blurred by sleep, Johnson answered and asked who it was. A second later, satisfied, he opened the door and was listening in stunned amazement to news that staggered belief. Lincoln murdered! God in heaven! With unashamed emotion, he gripped Farwell's hand and then flung both arms around his friend's shoulders.[76]

Outside in the corridor came the scurry and scuffle of many men and then there was another prodigious banging on the door. This was a guard hastily mustered by the excited hotel clerks. Soon it included a sprinkling of friends who had heard meager details of an almost unbelievable story. Armed with sword canes, clubs, and even drawn pistols, they came.

Stark chaos and bewilderment were depicted on everyone's face. Rumors swept over the gathering throng like a rain squall over a seascape. Presently, there came the thud of military feet on the stairs. Secretary Stanton, hiding like a scared rabbit from assassins himself, had nevertheless remembered to send a detachment of soldiers under command of Major James O'Beirne, of the Provost Guard, to take over the protection of Johnson. The Major brought last-minute news to clear away the rumors.

"The President is badly wounded, Mr. Johnson, but the doctors cannot say whether he will live or not. He is still unconscious. Secretary Seward has also been attacked. Both he and his son were badly stabbed. The assassins have escaped, but never fear, we will get them!"

Johnson hurriedly dressed himself and announced his determination to go to Lincoln's bedside at once. Friends did their best to deter him from leaving the safety of his room but the Tailor was insistent. Accompanied by the provost officer, Farwell, and a squad of soldiers, he set off for the Peterson residence. The streets were filled with excited people and his progress was slow. The time was about 2:00 A.M.[77]

In a middle room of the now famous old house across from the theater, he found Lincoln sprawled sidewise on a bed too short for his lanky form. The President was unconscious and his breath came in labored gasps. The room was crowded with people, members of the Cabinet, a sprinkling of congressmen, army men, and several doctors. Mrs. Lincoln stood at the head of the bed, sobbing violently; young Tad, open-eyed with wonder, was at her side.

The Radicals spread a tale that Johnson never visited Lincoln during his last hours. They said he had gone to bed too drunk to be awakened. Nothing was farthest from the truth. There is plenty of proof of his presence at Lincoln's bedside, none whatever to support the evil gossip of the Radicals. Currier and Ives issued an inaccurate colored print of the death scene in which Johnson was not shown, but they corrected this when their error was made known to them.[78]

At dawn the next morning a soft rain started falling over the city. The street before the theater and the Peterson house was thronged with people; their eyes anxiously centered on that doorway through which officials came and went. At 7:20, church bells all over the city started up a doleful peal. Lincoln was dead.

A few moments later, General Halleck, Charles Sumner, and several others climbed into the General's carriage and drove to the Kirkwood House to notify Johnson, officially, that he was now President of the United States and must take unusual precautions until his safety was assured. Three hours later, in the presence of a little group of Cabinet members and friends, he took the oath of office from Chief Justice Chase.

Visibly grief-stricken and depressed by the greatness of the high office so suddenly thrust upon him, he was, nevertheless, calm and master of himself. Rejecting Chase's help, he had prepared a brief statement of his acceptance of the presidency. Slowly, yet in a firm voice, he read it to the little group. It was simple and to the point. It indicated his great grief at the suddenness of events and his refusal to be stampeded into any statement of intentions. His administration must be developed by events of the future. He solemnly declared, "The only assurance I can give of the future is reference to the past."

As the Cabinet members filed out of the room, puzzled about their status, Johnson shook each one by the hand and begged him to remain at his task for the good of the Nation. Later that day, in an emergency session of the same body,

55

he made a blunder. He informed the Cabinet that his policy would be substantially that of Lincoln's and that he desired each Cabinet officer to continue his office—that he had no intention of making any changes.

He was to pay dearly for the mistake. With few exceptions, he should have asked for resignations and started his term with men friendly to himself and his plans. In the person of his Secretary of War, he, unknowingly at that moment, had acquired the greatest trouble-maker ever to enter his life.

For Edwin Stanton was one of the most despicable creatures ever to hold office in the government of the United States. Of honor he had none, of vanity no end, and it is to his everlasting shame that he was one of the prime causes of the troubles the conquered South was soon to undergo.[79]

"A spy under Buchanan, a tyrant under Lincoln and a traitor to Johnson, this man was as cruel and crafty as Domitian," wrote the son of President Taylor.[80]

An officeholder under Buchanan, he helped ruin that unhappy man's life and, once he had gone into retirement, turned around and became his paid spy for political purposes. In Lincoln's Cabinet his treachery reached new peaks. Under the guise of "war measures," he thrust bodyguards on Lincoln who were hardly more than spies engaged to report the President's every move.

The very porters who cleaned the White House were in his pay. They brought to him the contents of the wastepaper baskets that he might puzzle out things he wasn't party to. He had it so fixed that the terminal point for White House communications was in the war building offices. Before any message to Lincoln or his leading men could be delivered, it was read and studied by the Secretary.

Nursing secret hopes to fill the presidential chair some day, Stanton ingratiated himself into the counsels of the Radicals who were opposing Lincoln. Enforcing strict secrecy on other officials, he calmly kept certain senators advised of every secret move made at the White House or planned by the War Department.

Long before Lincoln's death, this strange man was already scheming how to nullify Lincoln's every hope and plan. The doctor's announcement of Lincoln's death found him plotting vigorously against his successor. Loyalty was never an attribute of Edwin M. Stanton.

On Capitol Hill the Radicals anxiously awaited Johnson's statement of intentions for his regime. Within a few moments after the Cabinet quit the Kirkwood parlors, news spread like wildfire among the Senators and Representatives eagerly waiting to take advantage of the National tragedy. Johnson's brief explanation of his plans was disconcerting. "Would have the same policy as Lincoln, eh? Mr. Johnson had another think coming if that was his program!" they chortled.

Lincoln's body had not yet stiffened in death before they were seething and frothing—planning how to get a bridle and a chain-bit on his iron-willed successor to office:[81] as well try to harness the sun.

But there was widespread belief on the Hill that Johnson would walk hand in hand with the Radicals in their plans for bleeding the South dry and perpetuating their political hold on all the people. Johnson had said little. His speech at the inaugural hadn't indicated his sentiments towards the South.

What gave hope to the Radicals were the biting words Johnson had uttered in his speech of acceptance in Nashville the previous fall. Hadn't he sworn to hang every traitor? Hadn't he taken a mighty oath to seize their lands and fortunes and divide them with the poor? Even now the whole country was wondering what Johnson's attitude would really be towards the South when the war was over. His fiery words had never been forgotten. The South trembled in fear lest he carry them out.

Despite the solemnity of the moment, the Radical leaders were too impatient to delay their plans because of Lincoln's death. As a matter of stark truth, his death was nothing short of a stroke of good fortune to them. They frequently visited Johnson to demand an outright statement of his plans for reconstruction. Charles Sumner, the effete, bombastic Senator from Massachusetts, delegated himself a committee of one to compel Johnson to show his hand.

Sumner found Johnson, early that evening of the day of Lincoln's death, in the Kirkwood parlors, sorrowfully discussing the tragedy with various callers. Tears were in

Johnson's eyes and on the faces of those around him, but Sumner never stopped for sentiment, decorum, or reverence. The Tailor stared at this pompous aristocrat of whom a wit jokingly had said, "He never even read the Bible because he hadn't written it!" Then he led his visitor to a little side room.

Sumner consumed almost an hour of his time harping on the subject of reconstruction. What did Mr. Johnson intend to do about it? Did he agree that the Negro must be instantly granted suffrage? Johnson listened and said little beyond the fact he would soon have something to say. He would not state himself definitely, but something in his manner gave the foolish Sumner hope that he would offer no trouble. Somewhat pleased and reassured, he took his leave to spend the evening writing to distant friends that he did not think they need to worry about Johnson![82]

Little did Sumner nor any other man understand Andrew Johnson! They now had a different man than the kindly, diplomatic Lincoln. Here was hardest steel to oppose them. Here was stubbornness such as they had never encountered before. Here was a man who would listen to anyone but, nevertheless, continue on his course—indifferent to advice if he felt he was right. Here was the rock against which their sordid plans to loot the helpless South were to batter in vain.

The next day, Sunday, Lincoln's body lay in state in the White House. Thousands of tearful people passed the bier. But that didn't prevent Edwin Stanton from calling a meeting in his office across the street, of the Radical leaders. Stealthily, he showed them a draft of HIS idea for the reconstruction of the southern states.

Later on that day, a file of soldiers were searching the Kirkwood Hotel, and especially Room 126, for a little, shaking, cringing creature named Atzerodt, who had been ordered to kill Johnson but who had lost his nerve the day before and became drunk. They found a pistol under his pillow. But the man wasn't there. They caught him a few days later, the 20th, in western Maryland. The soldiers who nabbed him were promised a reward of $25,000, but they never received a penny. The money was appropriated, but somehow it got into the wrong hands.

Atzerodt would hang, as an accessory for the murder of Abraham Lincoln. He had joined Booth's mad conspiracy, however, meaning only to kidnap and not to kill.

As Shakespeare sagely observed, mortals are fools with their supposed omnipotent plans. The Gods write the ending, to the utter confounding of assassins, scheming Radicals, and iron-willed Presidents.

CHAPTER 8

DESTINY SPINS HER WEB

One has only to ponder a moment or two to realize why Johnson's "single-track" mindedness was so essential at the moment. Everywhere there was turmoil and emotional crisis. Washington especially might well be described as bedlam, so varied and conflicting were the thoughts and actions of the mulitudes who filled its streets and packed its hotels and boardinghouses. The armies of the North were disbanding and thousands of men were suddenly thrown back on their own resources after rigid military discipline. To add to the confusion, innumerable ex-slaves poured into the city from southward. They were homeless, jobless, poverty-stricken, but in their simple minds was a tragic belief that now that slavery was ended their "Day of Jubilee" had come.

How people ate is a mystery; they slept wherever they could drop their bodies. From sidewalk counters, made from a plank or two resting on empty barrels, vendors dispensed food and drink to those unable to afford the regular restaurants and bars. Whiskey—if such it could be called—sold for a dime a drink and was served in tin cups filled directly from a barrel. No one seemed to care that the cups were never washed. Hawkers moved everywhere among the jostling, hawking crowds, dispensing peanuts, popcorn, milk, oysters, meat sandwiches, and hard-boiled eggs. There were dust, dirt, flies, and evil smells everywhere.[83]

The hotels, boardinghouses, and cafes were packed to capacity day and night. There were bars and gambling houses and places of ill fame by the score, and one and all were doing a land-office business. Public morals made their sacrifices to the God of War.

Up on the Hill, the electorate spouted in public and schemed in private. The chief topic of conversation among them, as with the public, was speedy vengeance for the base murderers of Mr. Lincoln and suitable punishment for the misguided southerners. Every man had his own scheme and even the Radicals disagreed among themselves, save on their desire to get Andy Johnson under their thumbs as soon as possible. Johnson very quickly discovered that he was surrounded by traitors, sycophants, and unscrupulous politicians who masked their greed under cries for vengeance. As Johnson indicated at his oath-taking, his policies would unfold as his administration developed. That was plain warning.

Until May 26, temporary headquarters were established for him in a little room next to the Secretary of the Treasury's office.[84] It was early June before Mrs. Lincoln, mentally aberrated by grief, was enabled to leave the White House. Until then, Johnson worked early and late, receiving delegations trying to lay some constructive plans. He was so busy that he had all his meals sent in by tray, and when he finally left for the day, it was usually late at night and bed-time.

Moving into the White House brought no relief from his arduous labors. Until the arrival of his wife and family, Johnson kept bachelor quarters with a vengeance. Lincoln had employed two secretaries—the pressure on Johnson forced him to use no less than six. Never before, nor since, perhaps, have men in the White House worked harder. The matters that required his attention seemed endless.

To consider them for a moment: thousands of officers were seeking discharge from or promotion in the service. Hundreds of others sought executive clemency for everything from criminal acts to departures from the stern rules and regulations of war times. Countless men from all over the land sought appointments in the new administration; they were irked to be told that Mr. Lincoln's appointments would stand. Former owners of confiscated property bedeviled him day and night for return of their possessions.

On May 29, Johnson had issued an amnesty proclamation, offering full pardon and restitution of all property except slaves to "all persons lately engaged in rebellion" who

61

would take an oath to support the Constitution and uphold all the laws. This proclamation, however, exempted certain individuals from its provisions—high officials of the late Confederate states, all officers over the rank of colonel, all officers who had been educated at West Point or Annapolis and who had resigned from the U. S. forces to enter the Confederate cause, and finally, all those whose estimated property value or net worth exceeded twenty thousand dollars.

The proclamation ended with a strange offer: anyone in the excepted classes could appeal directly to the President for clemency. Thus, Johnson brought down upon his head thousands of pardon-seekers. Why Johnson did not extend open pardon to southerners worth more than twenty thousand dollars is easy to explain. He felt the wealthy men of the South were guilty of rebellion. They were not entitled to the same treatment as the trusting masses. The Radicals viewed this as a sign of fitting severity leading to the confiscation of property. But they were wrong; Johnson merely planned a long probation for them to enforce the idea of future loyalty into their minds.[85]

Very early in Johnson's incumbency, someone discovered that, hard-boiled though he was with men, almost any woman could twist him around her finger. He couldn't resist a woman's tears or pleas. There then sprang up in Washington a group of women known as "pardon brokers," and they had no trouble getting clients. For several years, this horde of scheming, wheedling femininity descended upon the White House at all hours, seeking an audience with the harassed President. William Crooks has told that in the year between April 15, 1865, and June 15, 1866, Johnson issued 1,963 of these special pardons. They were not, however, instantly issued. In every case there was lengthy investigation ere Johnson made a final decision.[86]

To add to his labors there were trade restrictions to be removed from southern ports; tariffs and prohibitions to be weighed and pondered and made or unmade. There was a constant stream of visiting delegations from all over the land as well as from Congress. There were new foreign diplomats to be received, high-ranking army and navy officers returning from the field to make final reports or offer suggestions. Today, such pressure would never be tolerated upon the time of a Chief Executive. It soon wore Johnson out and he took to bed from what his physician said was "bilious fever."

All the while this vast activity was inundating the President and his assistants, the greater problem of how best to deal with the South was in his mind. To obtain firsthand information on the subject, he dispatched Chief Justice Salmon Chase on a tour of the southern states. He merely wanted timely information but Chase exceeded his authority. His tour became a heartless parade in which he did much gloating over a conquered foe. He also caused endless trouble by stirring up the simple Negroes and promising them everything from free education to suffrage to free plantations.[87] Hard on his heels, and sometimes with him, were Carl Schurz and a retinue of newspapermen.[88]

The South was a torn and complex society. An aristocracy was dying in fearful agony. There was ruin, chaos, and devastation everywhere and, unlike the joy and jubilance predominating in the North, only despair and stark grief filled the hearts of the South.

Sherman, in his march to the Sea, had spared nothing in the wide swathe he cut; homes, schools, churches, barns, hen-houses—everything habitable or useful—had been put to the torch, after being looted. His men had even hacked down the fruit trees and uprooted the berry bushes. Cattle and swine and poultry had been slaughtered to the very "seed" stock, lest the enemy eventually find sustenance. Other victorious northern generals had more or less patterned their activities along similar lines.

A wise, compassionate Lincoln had insisted of Grant that the surrender of Lee and his men must recognize their need for rehabilitation. At Appomatox, the Confederates were permitted to keep their horses and mules.

But horses and mules are scarcely enough when one must start up again from scratch. There were no seeds available—no reserve stores of such stark essentials as flour, meal, potatoes, and pork. The grocery-store shelves were bare, and there was no money. All the former currency had been transferred into Confederate issue for which there was no use. Thousands were dead. Women were alone. Some who had never labored were compelled to do the work which was formerly performed by slaves.

Perhaps it is well that history glosses over the real horrors and tribulations of those days; of man's inhumanity to his fellows. Here were fellow Americans, yet, thanks to a handful of greedy, rapacious, power-mad individuals, they would be treated with less mercy and charity than we have time and again shown to unknown millions starving in faraway Armenia or the Chinese victims of a Yangtze River flood.

Transportation was at a standstill; stores were closed; banks failed; insurance companies collapsed. Schools, churches, and colleges seemed like institutions of the past. Thousands of children grew to manhood with little or no education. In the once-flourishing ports, the wharves were crumbling from disuse; the roadsteads were destitute of shipping of any kind. The highways and byways were filled with thousands of footsore, weary, hungry soldiers, walking back to their homes. Some found their homes no longer existed, and nobody was left to give them news of friend or family. Many were suffering from wounds and others were cripples. One and all were hungry and sick.

The South had only one hope of getting back on its feet and avoiding starvation. That was to induce the former slaves to pitch in and help their old masters raise a crop until some suitable plan could be worked out for the good of all concerned.[89]

But the untutored black had temporarily decided he was through working in the fields. "Massa Lincoln and Ginral Grant had done gibben him his freedom so why work anymore?"[90] It didn't immediately dawn on them that the bacon, meal, and beans given to them by the Yankee invaders wouldn't last forever. Let the master hustle up his own corn, okra, and yams!

Thousands of former slaves did stand loyally by their masters and mistresses. For some, loyalties and habits of a lifetime weren't to be broken lightly by disaster.[91]

. The confusion was in no small measure inspired by agitators from the North, men in the employ of not only the

64

Radicals but also the Union League Clubs of New York and Philadelphia.

The Negro was to insist on immediate franchise. Once he got the vote, underhanded men meant to tell him how best to use it. Whether or not he ate or ever was given the former estates of his masters or an education meant not a thing to those agitators nor the master minds behind them.

Idleness, months of debauchery, and waiting for promises to be kept were having a sorry effect on the Negro. All over the South, former slaves were lording it over their former owners. In many places white Union troops were replaced by black regiments. Friction was spreading about the South like heat lightning.[92] That year saw a rush of race riots in Norfolk, New Orleans, and Richmond, from attempts by Negroes to remove the color line as was daily demanded by Charles Sumner, Thad Stevens, and others.[93]

The Nation was getting a preview of the next few years. But there was much disinterest. The war was over at last. Forget everything and celebrate. Let Congress and Mr. Johnson do the worrying.

Unfortunately, there were bigger issues in the background than the people could immediately see. Andrew Johnson was aware of them and so were his enemies.

The Radicals queried, would Johnson share the spoils with them or would he continue his foolishness about constitutional liberties?

The President would neither share graft with anyone nor was he forswearing the Constitution and his integrity as executive head of the people! He hoped to return reason to the country.

CHAPTER 9

ENTER THE VILLAINS

The humble people of the North fought and died in the Civil War on the theory that no state could leave the Union. Once the last Confederate soldier laid down his weapons, it was logical to expect a united nation would move forward again, binding up one another's wounds, as they fell into step.

Reconstruction became a horror. In reality, it was the battle between a corrupt, power-lusting, vindictive Congress and an honest, merciful President whose stubborn courage and resoluteness of purpose became the Rock upon which selfish ambitions were shattered in the end. It is an unfortunate thing that the real victims of this power struggle were proud fellow-Americans, unfortunate enough to have been on the losing side.

In his preface, Claude Bowers[94] says: "Andrew Johnson . . . fought the bravest battle for Constitutional liberty and the preservations of our institutions ever waged by an Executive . . . the unvarnished truth that vindicates him makes so many statues in our public squares and parks seem a bit grotesque."

If ever there was a war fought on this globe whose causes were utterly free of commercial taint and man's avarice for power or riches, then we have failed to learn about it. The Civil War was no exception and from the opening gun to the last, one is ever aware that here was a titanic struggle between the industrial North and the agrarian South. All too long, King Cotton had ruled the land and hard by its side stood the power of wheat and corn from the Central and far-western sections. With never a scruple, northern industrialists and financiers used the aftermath of the Civil War to further their selfish ends— ends they had fought for years to bring about through other measures.

The people of the United States didn't realize at the time, and few realize it today, but Reconstruction was sheerly and purely an artificial fog, behind which the "master-minds" staged the revolution that changed America from a democracy to a plutocracy of ever-growing magnitude. The age of machinery and "Big Business" and giant corporations had arrived. In northern and eastern big cities, millions of European immigrants were soon to suffer a worse form of slavery than ever their black brethren of the South had known.

This transition was the work of the many men, scarcely any of whom realized, let alone suspected, that they were but human marionettes acting at the bidding of such puppet-masters as Jay Cooke, James Fisk, Jay Gould, and others, who grew fabulously rich and powerful while their tools fought and bickered and plundered outrageously on their own account. Never before, nor since, in our history, have political morals fallen so low, nor men in high places been so notoriously dishonest and indifferent to their trust.[95]

Much of the corruption led back to Wall Street and the sanctimonious precincts of the Union League Clubs of New York and Philadelphia. From these "headquarters" went out the orders, not only to outstanding politicians, but to a bevy of men who were the propagandist of the day. In our own time we would call them public relation specialists, but in the Sixties an unsuspecting public knew them only as newsmen and cartoonists. Their task was to sell the northern public on the idea that only the Radical leaders in Congress stood between the national interest and the machinations of Andrew Johnson.

Johnson very quickly saw through this fog of deceit that was spreading throughout the land. In an interview, he openly declared that the war of finance is the next war we have to fight and he amplified his remarks by revealing that an aristocracy based on some two billion and a half of national securities had arisen in the northern states to assume that political control which the consolidation of great financial and political interests previously gave to the slave oligarchy.[96] Here was the real Andy again, battling against the aristocracy of wealth—no longer a southern, but now a northern aristocracy.

> We have all read history and is it not certain that of all aristocracies, that of mere wealth is the most odious, rapacious, and tyrannical. It goes for the last dollar the poor and helpless have got; and with such a vast machine as this Government under their control that dollar will be fetched.

> The aristocracy based on Negro property disappears at the southern end of the line, but only to reappear in an oligarchy of bands and national security in the States which suppressed the rebellion.

However pregnant and tremendous his words, the people failed to take them to heart, and with scarcely a protest, save from a few newspapers, the financiers and their political cohorts fattened themselves on the public treasury and made the excuse of Reconstruction a hollow alibi for unbelievable corruption and looting that was to continue almost without check for a generation. The sole effect of Johnson's warning was to bring down instantly upon his head the devastating enmity of the financial interests of the North.

They were too smart and too shrewd, however, to fight him in the open. Their method was ridicule and distrust —two unfailing and terrible weapons in the hands of the unscrupulous. With men like David R. Locke and Thomas Nast at their beck and call, they lampooned Johnson from one end of the land to the other. Locke, under the homely pseudonym of "Petroleum Nasby," convulsed the Nation with his barbed witticisms. Nast, like a picador at a bull-fight, devastated Johnson with cartoons that derided and belittled and undid his every decent effort. Remember, we scarcely had any libel laws in those days, nor was the Tailor the type of fighter who would have utilized them if they had been in force. He was too indifferent and too aware of his own goal in life to cling to such defenses.

Nast's tremendous power over the masses, through his amazing cartoons in *Harper's* and several newspapers, easily made him Johnson's outstanding enemy from the standpoint of widespread influence. Paine depicts him as sincere in his belief that Johnson was the enemy of the Nation and determined to restore the South to its old powers.[97]

It would take a volume to list the mere names of Johnson's actively working enemies, and it would take the pen of a Shakespeare to depict them in their true colors. Some men of the times did try to portray their enemies in the most vehement words in their vocabularies, but posterity has been cheated often by charitable editors who censored their remarks or even deleted them in full. McClellan, for example, described Secretary of War Stanton in the most unflattering light. He was a conspirator, overanxious for power and would stop at nothing to attain it. He was the chief stumbling block to the success of the Peninsular campaign and a backbiter of President Lincoln whom he described as an ape.[98]

Numerous other sources, however, give us a true picture of this vain, dishonorable, little popinjay, and if they are half as reliable as he proved the opposite, then he more richly deserved hanging than did the unfortunate Mrs. Surratt, for whose death he was responsible.

A private "tippler" and high-strung to the point where his own panic in the face of even the most minor ordeals, affected those around him, Stanton was easily the outstanding trial and tribulation of Johnson's and Lincoln's administration. As Attorney General in the closing days of Buchanan's tenure of office, Stanton helped ruin him politically, only to become his paid spy when Lincoln took over.

There isn't time to review his record here in the Civil War. It is enough to say that he did much to discredit Lincoln, and when the Union Party renominated him, Stanton's ego suffered a tremendous defeat, for he had vainly hoped for the nomination himself! Gideon Welles speaks of his chagrin in his diary.[99]

Why Johnson tolerated him so long is a major mystery. In fact, his continued retention of him gave rise to many ugly rumors. Time and again, pressure was brought upon him to oust Stanton and even petitions begging such action were sent to him. Stanton's spying and his betrayal of

69

Johnson's confidences to the Radical leaders may have fooled Johnson or possibly Johnson kept him close to watch him. Johnson seems to have been aware of Stanton's activities.

A few years ago, the Library of Congress, coming into possession of several shorthand books left by Colonel William G. Moore, one of Johnson's secretaries, had them transcribed. Under date of May 2, 1867, Moore had pothooked an entry of more than passing interest: "The President expressed the belief today that had it not been for the War Department, all our troubles would long since have been healed. He said he was convinced that that department had thrown every obstacle in the way of the consummation of his plans for restoration."

Stanton's true position in the assassination of Abraham Lincoln has never been fully disclosed, nor adequately covered. There is some evidence that Stanton's spies, of whom he had a goodly number, had warned him long in advance of the plot first to abduct Lincoln, which was frustrated, and then to murder him. Stanton's undercover men seem to have even apprised him of the names of members of the gang and where they congregated. Ben Ames Williams, in his startling book, *Mr. Secretary,* goes so far as to imply that Stanton received notes from the gang in advance of their plans, their information going to him on the assumption that he approved of their plans and would help them! Mr. Williams does not indicate the source of his statements. They cannot be checked.[100] But a recent historian, Theodore Roscoe, again recasts the aura of mystery and suspicion about Lincoln's Secretary of War.

The fact does remain that Booth, who could easily have been taken alive, was shot dead, the inference being that somebody wanted his mouth sealed. It is also thought that Booth's diary was badly mutilated by Stanton. Also, that he deliberately removed the military court's recommendation for clemency for Mrs. Surratt when they sent their findings to Andrew Johnson for the execution of the conspirators. Not knowing this, Johnson signed her death warrant and, within a week, the Nation was hurling murder charges at him. In reality, Stanton was the murderer.

Down on Capitol Hill, Johnson had two other outstanding enemies, but, unlike the War Secretary, this pair at least sometimes fought him openly and made no secret of their enmity, once Johnson made his position clear. A more oddly assorted twain would be difficult to imagine, yet their common battle drew them together and made them close.

In the Senate, Charles Sumner, of Massachusetts, held the spotlight as leader of the Radicals and the outstanding Abolitionist of the country. An evil genius of the first water, Sumner almost baffles characterization. His colleagues detested him, but those who only heard him speak, or met him once, were strangely drawn by his deep, sonorous voice and his blase, worldly mannerisms.

Most other Congressmen despised him because they knew him so well. To outsiders, he sparkled like a real diamond, but closer scrutiny revealed him as "paste." Arrogant, pompous, and overbearing, he openly regarded as fools all men who failed to agree with him. His vanity was something to whistle over and a visit to England in his formative years had done strange things to his mind and personal habits. Ever after, he dressed like an Englishman and tried to pretend he was one. He never condescended to talk "with" people, but always "down" to them.

Those who didn't know him well considered him an intellectual of the first rank. His speeches were flavored with quotations from four languages and couched in flowery eloquence. He fancied himself an American Cicero. An omnivorous reader, he remembered everything.[101]

He was the foremost champion of the Negro. His entire career in the Senate was devoted to fighting for the franchisement of the humble black; in demanding equal rights for him and otherwise fighting his battles. His fight against Johnson was almost solely because he believed Johnson favored slavery.

Sumner's attitude toward the Negro was strange. He couldn't stand to be near him. He was a theorist, a principle maker on the question. He possessed no great love of the Negro.[102]

Over on the House side—spinning strange webs and

71

thundering and bellowing like some archangel—was the strangest individual ever to disgrace the American scene, Thaddeus Stevens, of Pennsylvania, Chairman of the Ways and Means Committee and acknowledged Czar of the House.

Neither Dante, Dore, nor Poe in their wildest moments ever conceived a mythical character like Stevens. Club-footed, tall, cadaverous, bald as a bone when minus his wig, and beetle-browed, he was a driver of men and they fled before him to do his bidding because his venomous, biting words were more hurtful than leaden whips. They obeyed him through sheer fear of his tongue and threat of ruin.[103]

An inveterate gambler, drunkard, and sexualist, he seemed to possess but one virtue—he neither hid his faults nor denied them. He sneered when men exposed Miss Smith, his mulatto housekeeper, as his common mistress. It was nationally known that when her husband, a barber, passed away, she promptly moved in with him. When he finally died, of tuberculosis, Stevens had himself buried in a Negro cemetery and there, by his side, after her death, they laid the mulatto "lady."

Stevens was known as the "Great Commoner." Possessed of a brilliant, yet twisted mind, his whole life seems to have been actuated by hate. He hated poverty. He had been born to it. He hated the South. In his narrow view, the section was hateful and purge worthy. He saw it as a land of despicable aristocrats to whom democracy was a mere word and who held both black and poor white as chattels. No democrat himself, he yet was a leveler beside which Jean Jacques Rousseau appeared as a constructive statesman.

He hated the South the more because Confederate soldiers had raided his home town of Lancaster and burned his iron foundry, destroying his first fortune, earned by practicing law.

His second fortune came as a Member of Congress—the result of huge fees earned for legislative advice and actions. In these days we use the term "graft," but during Stevens' tenure of office, fellow Members regarded it as a prerogative of their position. If Andrew Johnson hadn't been so stubborn, Stevens would have garnered a great deal more money than he did, and part of his vicious hate of Johnson was due to this fact.[104]

All the other Radicals who played their part in bleeding the South dry and withholding mercy from her were mere jackals and knaves.

CHAPTER 10

PRELUDE TO TRAGEDY

The Congress, chosen to lead the North during the war, had been elected sheerly to prosecute the conflict. The oftener they damned the Rebels and waved the Bloody Shirt, the more their constituents cheered and voted for them. There were few, if any, humanitarian or noble-hearted men in either House during or immediately following the conflict. The post-war Congress screamed for vengeance. It was part of their vote-getting tactics.

When Abraham Lincoln pleaded for compassion and begged the victors swiftly to bind up the Nation's wounds, his words only brought forth sneers and expressions of rage and hate, that is—from most Members of Congress.

In his annual message to Congress, December 8, 1863, and by proclamation of the same date, Lincoln tentatively outlined his plans for Reconstruction by reciting what he had already done in that direction in Louisiana and Arkansas, now completely in Northern hands. He had issued a proclamation putting the state of Louisiana under a military governor. When ten per cent of a state's population had taken a Federal oath, then they could elect a new legislature, a governor, and national representatives. All citizens, save high-ranking Confederates, were to take the oath of allegiance to the United States; the new legislature was to repudiate all Confederate debts and to emancipate all slaves.[105]

The committee on the conduct of the war heard this merciful proposal with hearts and minds steeled in another quarter. When Louisiana complied with the President's proclamation and sent two Members to Congress in June, 1863, they were admitted. Arkansas, greatly heartened by this, followed suit and hopefully sent their new Senators and Representatives to Washington. Up rose Charles Sumner with a resolution to block their admission. Had they given the franchise to the slaves and made them their equal? No! Well, what greater proof that Arkansas was still in a state of "being out of the Union"? The resolution was sent to committee for action.

On June 27, 1864, the Senate Judiciary Committee finally deigned to consider the vexatious matter. By a vote of 27 to 6, the new Members were rejected on the grounds they came from conquered states not now in the Union! Quickly the House passed a similar bill rejecting the new Members "until both Houses could pass suitable laws covering the readmission of all states lately engaged in rebellion."

That action was the opening gun in the battle against Lincoln's plans for a merciful solution of the Reconstruction problem. It was to become the unhappy lot of Andrew Johnson to carry on the fight of his chief.

On July 2, 1864, both Houses passed a bill making "suitable provisions" for the reorganization and readmission of rebellious states along extreme lines: the Wade-Davis bill. It embodied the amazing provision that the President, after obtaining consent of Congress, "shall admit and recognize the state governments so established." It disfranchised all who had taken up arms against the United States and required a majority of the population to take the oath before the establishment of civil government could be accomplished.[106]

July 4th, the day Congress was to adjourn, Lincoln arrived at the Capitol with his Cabinet to sign the numerous bills awaiting executive approval. When the Wade-Davis bill was handed him, he calmly laid it aside and went on with other matters, while tense Radical Members hovered about him. Finally their concern became too great and Zack Chandler persisted that he sign it. Lincoln rebuked him with the statement that it was placed before him just a few moments before Congress adjourned, that it was of doubtful constitutionality, and it was too important a matter to be hastily acted on. This action was a matter of parliamentary law and the over-anxious Radicals, by waiting until the very last hour, gave Lincoln an opportunity to pocket veto the bill. He had won his point, but he had infuriated his enemies. More than ever they were determined to have their will.[107] There followed the vicious Wade-Davis Manifesto.

The lines of battle were already and clearly drawn for Johnson. Lincoln's brutal assassination affected Johnson just as it had all other loyal-minded citizens. The immediate response was anger, rage, and a quick vengeance. Until most of the details were learned, there were many wild tales charging the whole affair to various southern leaders. So, under the strain of the moment, it was perhaps natural for Johnson to loom up in the people's eyes as an avenger. The Radical leaders exulted; the South trembled and prepared for the worst.

But Johnson was no bloodthirsty leader unable to distinguish between justice and vengeance. With the execution of the co-conspirators of Booth and the lamentable inclusion of Mrs. Surratt in their number, both he and the Nation began to cool down. It wasn't long before he learned how Stanton and Judge Holt had tricked him in the matter of withholding the recommendation of leniency for Mrs. Surratt and presently the whole affair leaked out over the country. It had a sobering effect on everybody but the Radicals.

Secretary Seward played more than a little part in softening Johnson's heart and making him realize more clearly what had been in Lincoln's mind. After his grief died down, Johnson meditated on Lincoln's last words to the members of his Cabinet, held only a few hours before his death. No accurate transcription of this session seems to have been kept, and Gideon Welles failed to include them in his *Diary*. But, in 1872, Welles wrote a magazine account of that last meeting, and we quote a portion of it here:

> The President said he proposed to bring forward that subject [i.e., a rough draft of a plan for Reconstruction, prepared by Secretary Stanton] although he had not had time as yet to give much attention to the details of the plan, but it was substantially, in the general scope, the plan we had sometimes talked over in Cabinet meetings. We should probably make some modifications, provide further details; there were some suggestions which he should wish to make, and he desired all to bring their minds to the question, for no greater or more important one could come before us or any future Cabinet. He thought it PROVIDENTIAL that this great rebellion was crushed just as Congress had adjourned, and there were NONE OF THE DISTURBING ELEMENTS OF THAT BODY TO

HINDER AND EMBARRASS US. If we were wise and discreet, we should reanimate the states and get their government in successful operation, with order prevailing and the Union reestablished BEFORE CONGRESS CAME TOGETHER IN DECEMBER. This he thought important. We could do better, accomplish more without them. There were men in Congress who, if their motives were good, were nevertheless impracticable, and who possessed feelings of hate and vindictiveness in which he did not sympathize and could not participate. Each House of Congress, he said, had the undoubted right to receive or reject Members, the Executive had no control in this matter. But, Congress HAD NOTHING TO DO WITH THE STATE GOVERNMENTS, which the President could recognize and under existing laws, treat as other states, give the same mail facilities, collect taxes, appoint judges, marshals, collectors, etc., subject of course, to confirmation. There WERE MEN WHO OBJECTED TO THESE VIEWS, BUT THEY WERE NOT HERE AND WE MUST MAKE HASTE TO DO OUR DUTY BEFORE THEY COME HERE![108]

Weigh those words carefully. They are proof that, more than most men, he realized that the biggest task ahead was to restore the Union with the least amount of humiliation possible. Vengeance and punishment were as far from his mind as the poles are apart. He also knew full well the impossibility of getting suitable support and help from a Congress as vengeful and varied as the one then in power. To quote Edmund G. Ross, the courageous Senator of the period: "No such responsibility, no such herculean task, had ever before, in the history of civilization, devolved upon any ruler or political party.[109]

We thus have the prologue now to the scene as Johnson entered it with the untimely death of Abraham Lincoln. He walked out upon it almost alone, but the whole Nation would have been at his back had it only been permitted to understand the real issue involved.

CHAPTER 11

THE TAILOR SHOWS HIS COLORS

The Radicals were worried and apprehensive that summer and early fall of 1865. Andrew Johnson wasn't behaving in the least the way they believed he would. Northern extremists were looking in vain for the gibbets from which they hoped to see the southern leaders swinging. As for the prostrate South, a ray of hope gleamed fitfully over her desolate fields and towns. Perhaps this successor to Lincoln wasn't nearly as bad as they had been led to believe.

Truth is, the Tailor of Greeneville was proving himself utterly opposite to the man who had so recently startled the Nation with his tirades against traitors and treason. Mindful of Lincoln's adjurations to get Reconstruction under way before the "disturbing elements of Congress" returned in December, Johnson had quickly issued his amnesty and North Carolina proclamations near the end of May. The effect throughout the country was electric.

A sober, puzzled, grief-stricken Nation had watched Johnson take over his office. The press had led them to believe other things of this forceful, resolute man. Now that he stood revealed to them, however, they applauded and approved. The press, in the main, followed suit. Congratulatory letters flowed into the President from all over the country. Newspapers waxed eloquent in their praise. Even European capitols approved of his inclinations towards mercy and a swift reuniting of the country.

Nor was this all in Johnson's favor. All his life he had stood for economy in government and the end of the war found him able to prove his theories to the delight of the taxpayer —high and low. With incredible swiftness, he brought bureau after bureau, required by the war, to a swift ending. Their purpose was over. The Nation no longer needed them. By June his economies were reducing government expenditures by no less than ONE MILLION DOLLARS A DAY!

With relentless purpose and energy, he purged the civil lists of hundreds of supernumeraries and idlers, and their cries of rage only filled the taxpayers' hearts with glee. "Good Old Andy!" they cried enthusiastically. Swiftly, too, he began reducing the huge naval and military establishments. With never a bit of trouble, thousands of soldiers and sailors and late war prisoners were returned to their homes. Peace-time industry slowly got into gear again throughout the East and North. During his administration there was no economic letdown which follows a major war.

Even the high cost of living was somewhat reduced. Inventions poured into the Patent Office; foreign trade greatly increased, and the people once again took up the movement westward. They had been vigorous in war; they were now vigorous in peace.[110]

That the country appreciated him was proved by the thousands of letters which poured in on the hard-working President and his secretariat, to say nothing of the countless delegations and individuals who appeared in person to demand his time. It was sometime during that first summer that a group of New Yorkers was dumbfounded to have returned to them a magnificent carriage with four finely matched horses which they had tried to present to the President.

From Lancaster, Old Thad Stevens watched these things with brooding eyes. From Ohio, Benjamin F. Wade wrote to Charles Sumner, on June 14, 1865, "If something isn't done, the President will be crowned King before Congress meets! So much success will reconcile the people to anything."[111]

He then went on to suggest that the Massachusetts leader start something there that would help determine the growing popularity of Johnson throughout the country. Sumner had already started the ball rolling in a strange and uncalled-for manner. On June 1, he had been asked to deliver an eulogy to Lincoln at a huge memorial service held in Boston. Alas! Lincoln's name or virtues were hardly mentioned. Instead, his astounded audience heard a savage diatribe demanding instant enfranchisement for the late slaves! It was in bad taste and had instant repercussions.[112]

79

Thad Stevens boiled over with rage at these setbacks. His own influence was only great when he was surrounded by men whom he could acidly tonguelash. Desperately, he finally addressed a letter to the President from Philadelphia early in July: "I have not found a single person who approves of your policy! Wait for Congress!"[113]

By the time of his address on the state of the Union, December, 1865, much of what he had in mind had been accomplished. To continue military rule was impossible. Proclamations of amnesty were therefore issued upon which Southerners, with few exceptions, would be restored to citizenship. Beginning with North Carolina, May 29, 1865, the President appointed provisional governors who launched the political program placing the state on a constitutional footing. With orderly civil government effected, troops were removed and the transition from rebellions to peace made complete. The work was done quietly, efficiently, and the governors, under presidential orders, took on a tone of co-operation and friendliness.

Johnson's program, so bitterly resented by the Radicals, ought not to have surprised them. It had been fully discussed by the Cabinet, not one of whom expressed a single doubt about the executive's right to reorganize the formerly rebellious state governments. But it was a peculiar, abnormal period in American history when the powers possessed by one branch of government were looked upon with loathing by the others, and the Radicals were guilty of attempted usurpation. Moderate Congressional leadership could have prevented tragedy.[114] But there was none. There was only mediocrity, no great figure to ally with the President.

So many things happened in quick succession that fateful summer that it is difficult to mention them all, leastwise give them in the chronological order of their importance. The things to remember, however, are that Johnson was working at superhuman speed and endurance, to restore the Nation from an armed camp to one of peace and industry. If that wasn't enough, then there was the ghastly problem of uniting the states with mercy and compassion against the wishes of the Radical cohorts.

The cabal against Johnson meant to bring about delays and confusion until Congress would reconvene in December. With this end in view, they held numerous consultations with the tricky Stanton. Through his office, they "persuaded" the President to send Carl Schurz on a special tour of inspection of the southern states. Once he turned in his eye-witness report, it would be possible to make some truly wise plans for Reorganization! The scheme was for Schurz to dilly and dally until late November. Then Congress, returning, could demand his special report to the President.

Johnson stupidly permitted the tour. He was mistaken. Schurz, a German nationalist of 1848, who considered the attempt at dismemberment of the Union the highest of political sins, went southward specifically looking for trouble, not yet difficult to find. His report was clever. He spoke of conditions of quietude. But he added that southerners were not cleansed of treason and that they looked upon Negro suffrage with doubts. He made it seem as though the South was taking advantage of the President's "easy" reconstruction methods.[115] The Radicals would give wide publicity to Schurz's views.

The President didn't mind sending Carl Schurz, the German political refugee, on his mission, for it was a cheap way to get rid of him for the time being. He did refuse, however, to restore him to his former rank and pay as a Brigadier General, despite the little man's protests. Expense money he could have, but no more. So, the upshot was that Charles Sumner and Secretary Stanton privately financed him through the aid of a New York newspaper.

Andrew Johnson was erroneously very little concerned with the sort of report Carl Schurz might make to him on southern conditions.

Johnson already had dispatched other individuals into the South. Some went forth under the glare and white light of nationwide publicity. Others traveled secretly, with open minds and eyes, and you may depend on it, theirs were the reports the President trusted. Such an investigator was his faithful Secretary, Major Benjamin C.

Truman, who observed conditions favorably. Johnson's plan of reconstruction had a good effect.

The disbanded Confederate army was the sinews upon which a good rehabilitation could be based. "To the . . . regiments of the Rebel army, both officers and men, I look with great confidence as the best and altogether the most hopeful element of the South, the real basis of reconstruction and the material of worthy citizenship."[116] Others were equally observant and impressed, one being no less than Harvey M. Watterson, father of the man destined to become a great newspaper editor in Louisville—Henry Watterson.

Chase also was observing and reporting and betraying not only Johnson but the very South itself.[117] He coveted the presidency, and his treatment of his Negro audiences was meant to gain their vote! His letters to his famous daughter, Kate Chase Sprague, reveal his mind as a microscope does an unwelcome germ.[118] As for the Negroes, they promptly forgot his visit in the swift course of events.

Johnson's other sources of information about the true situation in the South were of the most competent kind: the reports that came to him personally from his military governors and the leaders of the various military units scattered throughout the conquered areas. With scarcely an exception, these men were opposed to Negro suffrage and there was grave reason for their views and warnings.[119]

From this, and his experience in Tennessee, Johnson sincerely believed that at the moment few Freedmen were ready for such responsibility. They were property-less; slavery had held them not only uneducated but illiterate and ill-informed. So many years kept from responsibility, they did not yet realize the cares of enlightened citizenship. One only needs to point out that aliens are not granted citizenship without a waiting period, which everyone agrees is sound policy—and yet such people are free and most of them literate.

Could only reason prevail in both the Radicals and the executive. An embittered protagonist of Johnson, Welles would write acridly of the Radicals and Charles Sumner: "Prominent men are striving to establish a party on the basis of equality of races in the Rebel States, for which people are not prepared. . . . . Mr. Sumner, who is an unmarried man, has striven to overcome what seems a natural repugnance"— Radical equality.[120]

On the other hand, Johnson's stubbornness caused him to lose political acumen, which he had so well evidenced as pre-war governor of Tennessee. When northern visitors asked him about his suffrage and reconstruction policies, he angrily turned and said, "Good Day, Gentlemen," and disappeared into the White House. The art of public relations was tragically lost in him.[121] He repeatedly failed to inform the public of his view that the intelligent black should possess the vote. Then, in the heat of the battle between him and Congress, he discarded this statesman-like policy. He came to view universal suffrage as a danger, leading to Civil War between the poor white and the Negro.[122]

The brother of General W. T. Sherman also judged that the Negro was not yet ready to vote, but he held to the contention that the Radicals were entitled to the power that their political representation would bring.[123]

General Grant was also aware of the Negroes' unreadiness for the ballot privilege, and he contended that those who still talked of punishment for southerners were heartless and unfeeling. His Generals in the field were candid in their personal reports to him. In their opinion, they contended the Negro begged for suffrage because he thought it meant the right to live in idleness and be fed by the government.[124]

What the new historians, who have "re-evaluated" the period, fail to realize is the lamentable condition of the freedmen during reconstruction, played upon, as poor pawns of the power politicians, by the Radicals. These unfortunates of the nineteenth are not the responsible Negroes of the twentieth century.

As we have seen, following the North Carolina and Amnesty proclamations, Johnson was utterly inundated for a little while with letters and wires of approval. Very soon, too, there was a series of party conventions—Democratic, Republican, and Union, endorsing his plan and forwarding laudatory resolutions. Everywhere, outstanding newspapers were printing such things as "proving himself a sagacious statesman," or "a discreet, merciful, clear-sighted, upright leader," and again and again eulogizing "his patriotism and unblemished loyalty."

This acclaim came from every section of the land. Also, there was scarcely a Governor, North, West, or East, who did not write a personal tribute.

The Radicals watched these signs with ill-concealed rage and, time and again, they met in secret conclave to plan ways to stop the growing tide. In the meanwhile, from the lounge-rooms of the New York and Philadelphia Union League Clubs, there sped away on furtive missions throughout the unhappy South more than one man entrusted with some sordid scheme in connection with the coming industrial "revolution." They were the forerunners of the carpetbaggers.

Along about June 1, 1865, Johnson was making another of his tragic mistakes. Up to that time, one of his ablest and truest counsellors had been Thomas Ewing, of Ohio. From him, the President had sought and gained much sound, solid, and worthwhile advice. But he turned to another advisor in the person of Jeremiah Sullivan Black. With cunning words, Black led him into situations where he was promptly "bushwhacked" and betrayed by his enemies. There would come a day when Johnson was to find Black out and forbid him the White House, but that day came too late to spare him ignominy and hurt.

The South was to embarrass Johnson too. The newly created legislatures were in no mood to accord unusual privileges to their late slaves. The section was willing to pass the thirteenth amendment but surely, they reasoned, that was enough for the North to demand of them.

Some of the North did want more, and were prompt to express themselves. They insisted on equal rights for everyone, regardless of color. They insisted on other things which several northern states themselves denied to the Negro—such as common schools, common cafes, meeting places, and equal employment opportunities.

Eager though they were to get Reconstruction over with,

consistent with the President's proposals, southern leaders were entirely too familiar with their late slaves than to grant terms of equality.

Already this "outlook" on life was beginning to harass the southerners in their herculean efforts to repair the havoc of war and survive. The Negro refused to work. Why should he? Hadn't the Yankees promised him everything from forty acres and a mule to a Golden Harp? He wouldn't work, but to live, he had to eat, and so in his new state of mental intoxication, he had to beg, steal, or else go without. Homeless, yet joyous and confident in freedom, they tramped the countrysides, striving always to locate themselves as close to a Federal army commissary department as possible. There, they could beg rations.

The situation was fast getting out of hand and rapidly becoming a source of constant tension and worry. In mutual self-protection, therefore, among the very first acts of the newly created southern legislatures was the framing of so-called "Black Codes." These were pretty much "work or else" edicts, and they awakened no end of furor in the North. *The Chicago Tribune,* for example, commenting on some of these laws, reminded the South what Yankee bayonets had done in the past, and threatened to turn one state (Mississippi) into a frog-pond unless she accorded her new citizens better treatment.

For the most part, the codes represented an attempt to bring order where there had been chaos. Some were enlightened, as in Georgia. Louisiana and Mississippi were unseemly harsh. Commonly, the states designated the freedmen as persons of color, and they were legally assigned certain civil rights. But they were not permitted to carry weapons, and their labor contracts were subject to severe enforcement. Laws against vagrancy were also hard.

States like Mississippi caused Johnson chagrin. Such codes smacked of the old chattel-owner relationship and attempted to channel the Negro's labor into husbandry, farm or domestic service. These gave Stevens and Sumner grist for their propaganda mills. And the unknowing northerner thought that all the codes presaged a return of the black to slavery.[125]

The unhappy southerners were caught "between the devil and the deep blue sea." Well they knew, and so did the commanding officers of the armies of occupation, that the Negro question was at best a difficult and most peculiar one. To add to the woes of the South, there was a constant disbandment of the Federal troops in their midst, and upon them they had depended for order. The white soldiers wanted to return home and get back to families and their work. Result—Negro troops who had nowhere to go remained in the Army and were stationed everywhere to terrorize and annoy and intimidate their former masters.[126] Truly, it was an unhappy situation. In sheer self-protection, then, the newly created legislatures sought and obtained Johnson's permission to re-establish state militias. This caused apprehension in some northern quarters and howls of rage in others. The Radicals, as they did with the Black Codes, were quick to turn this to their good account.

The middle of August, 1865, was a happy moment in Johnson's tense, overworked life. On a hot day, after endless delays, he was reunited with Eliza and his family. Many months had gone by since last he had seen them, and now he was in his glory to be surrounded by wife, son, daughters, sons-in-law, and merry grandchildren. Those grandchildren gave not only their stern *Granpere* a new lease on life, but the very somberness of the White House changed as well. Now it rang with the voices of children, a new homelike atmosphere prevailed. For once, the overworked President began eating rightly again and taking a recreational period down the river, or else in Rock Creek Park. Johnson had been ill that first summer and his condition caused more than a little concern to his friends and doctor. An old gall-bladder ailment put him to bed and, forever afterwards, twisted his face in lines of pain.

Washington society had viewed the Tailor's ascendancy to the White House with considerable misgivings. His humble origin had been too much to forgive and his life so far had been remote from the usual Capitol social functions. Now they flocked to the mansion to pay their respects and meet the First Lady and her family. They came prepared to laugh, and scorn, but they went away refreshed and delighted with a type of simple, straight-forward hospitality they were unaccustomed to. Speedily, the city forgot its laughter when the story went around that Mrs. Johnson had installed a cow at the White House to ensure plenty of pure, fresh milk for her family.

Meanwhile, the Radicals lost no opportunity to make demands upon Johnson that he insist on immediate fran-chisement for the hapless blacks. Sumner, for an example, with a great fanfare, sent a petition signed by three hundred Georgia Negroes, demanding the vote without delay.

The President, however, refused to be stampeded by these demands. Patiently he explained time and again that there was no law permitting an executive to tell any state who it should permit to vote. That was a matter for the states, and Johnson was a stickler for such things. Johnson might well have reminded the Radicals that suffrage was denied the Negro in all but six of the northern states and that until they set an example in their own bailiwick, they showed poor judgment demanding such things of the struggling South.

In his selection of provisional governors, Johnson had picked mostly outstanding members of the old Southern Whig Party. He had a definite reason for this choice, feeling that zealous members of the discredited Unionist minority, most of whom had never approved of the rebellion, would lend greater co-operation in restoring stable government. He had especially requested that his governors avoid the appointment or aid in the election of high Confederate officials to office.

Unfortunately, this proved an impossibility for the reason that almost everyone worthy of public office had played some part in the strife. Now, returned to civil life and des-perately seeking economic stabilization for themselves and their people, these former leaders found it impossible to sit back idle among the chaos about them. So, it was obvious that elections and appointments placed men in office whom the Radicals could point to with suspicion.

An example of these new elections can be briefed in a sentence or two. Georgia had elected to the United States Senate no less a personage than Alexander Stephens, late

Vice-President of the Confederacy, while the new Governor of Mississippi had been a Brigadier General. All in all, Congress was soon to be asked to accept as Members, four ex-Confederate generals, five ex-colonels, six members of the late Confederate Cabinet, and fifty-eight Congressmen, none of whom was able to take Johnson's oath of allegiance! Small wonder the Radicals were able to perturb the North with the question: "Last year men sought to destroy this nation. Now they wish to govern it! Dare we trust them?"

All this was part of the burden Johnson had to bear. Some of these high Confederates he pardoned, notably Stephens, with whom he had several long talks. It is a matter of record that Stephens, aside from his brief and unfortunate connection with the Confederacy, proved himself a loyal American, and had been consistently doubtful of secession as a cure for southern ailments.

That ominous, terrible summer slipped by with its various settings, scenes, and characters shifting almost momentarily. On November 13, 1865, South Carolina became the first of the southern states to announce she had complied with Johnson's reconstruction requirements. She had elected suitable officials, repudiated secession and the Confederate debt, and, chief of all, had ratified the 13th Amendment. On December 1, North Carolina completed its own house-cleaning task; Georgia and Alabama swiftly followed on December 6, and the 2nd, respectively. It was April of the following year, however, before Texas met all the requirements. And the Secretary of State was able to proclaim to the Nation that the war had officially ended. In the meanwhile, he was enabled to announce as early as December 18, 1865, that three-fourths of the states had now ratified the 13th Amendment and, henceforth, slavery was forever stamped out in America. The Nation went joyously mad for a few brief days.

Up from the South in early winter came Carl Schurz, his arrival timed by the Radicals to meet their plans. With highly inflated ego, he presented himself to Johnson and announced himself ready to write his report on true conditions in the South. The President read him at a glance—even "insulted him," according to the dapper little German, and bade him forget a written report. Nevertheless, Schurz turned out a voluminous document. The President, forced to submit it to Congress, also gave them Grant's view of the South in which the General advised not to humiliate the beaten section.[127]

In the wings, on the other side of the stage, waiting for his cue to enter, sat Thad Stevens. Carefully, he had rehearsed his lines and studied out his part.

With the opening of Congress, he had himself carried to its session where for a brief span he was to become the most powerful and dangerous individual in all the land.

CHAPTER 12

RECIPE FOR VILLAINY

"If I could be instrumental in restoring the government to its former relations and see the people once more united, I should feel that I had more than filled the measure of my ambition. If I could feel that I had contributed to this in any degree, my heart would be more than gratified and my ambition fulfilled."[128]

So said the President, October 13, 1865, to a visiting delegation of South Carolinians, and they left the White House agreeably impressed with a man who understood their vexatious problems and only wished to co-operate with everyone concerned.

Meanwhile, venomous and tricky as a Green Mamba snake, Thad Stevens arrived in Washington on December 1, 1865. There was in his cold, merciless mind a plan, which, properly executed, would tumble "King Andy" from his throne. It is a pity his biographers have not left us more data about where he had spent the last week in November, and with what individuals. We do know, however, that some of this time had been spent in the Union League Club in Philadelphia. There he had undoubtedly conferred with the financiers who pledged him support.[129]

Slowly the Radical plans matured for the defeat of everything Lincoln and Johnson had so sagely and mercifully planned. Desperately they were hunting for a policy they could "sell" to the Nation and as the summer waned and Johnson grew in national popularity their rage boiled over. All they could do, seemingly, was to counsel delay until Congress could meet again and seize the reins.

Some of the letters that were exchanged are astounding admissions of their knavery and double-dealing. They are found in profusion in the Sumner Manuscripts.[130] Delay, delay, on one ground or another, until the devils are civilized! beseeched Senator Chandler in one of these frank epistles; "the only hope I have is to gain time for suffering to do its work!"

Delay Presidential reconstruction! What cared the Radicals that the South was recovering under Johnson's guidance.

Propaganda has been a favorite device of scheming mankind since the world began, but it reached a new high in the United States the moment Andrew Johnson made clear to the Radicals that his policy was to be one of mercy and compassion. Overnight, a veritable army rose against him and their number was swollen by malcontents he had removed from office in his drive for economy.

Almost overnight, a small horde of newspapermen, hack writers, lecturers, and others were employed to strike back at him. Newspapers devoted to the Radicals' cause appeared like magic in the leading cities. All over the country, men were poised and ready to begin their attack the moment the order came.

Stevens launched into action the moment he arrived in Washington. That same night he held a secret meeting with some thirty of the leading Radical Senators and Representatives, already on the scene. Fiercely and savagely, he whipped them into a madness almost akin to his own. He pledged them that they would oppose all of Johnson's measures; that they would not seat a single Member from the newly reorganized states UNTIL BOTH HOUSES WERE IN COMPLETE AGREEMENT!

The next day the regular Republican Caucus was held and most of those present were unaware that Stevens and his gang had tricked them at the meeting the day before with an agreement. Swiftly and without opposition, Stevens was elected Chairman of a committee of fifteen to consider what was to be done with the southern Representatives, and which would direct Radical reconstruction. It was the work of a moment for him to offer his resolution, devised the previous day. Unaware that they were being "framed," the caucus voted the resolution unanimously.

December 4, 1865, saw an amazing scene enacted in the Capitol. As densely packed galleries watched with bated breath, the clerk called the roll, omitting the name of every new Member from the southern states, even Tennessee being included in the shutout. Bristling with rage, loyal Horace Maynard strode forward to present his certificate from Governor Brownlow. The clerk ignored him, and the House refused his plea for a hearing.

Brooks, of New York, the Minority Leader, tried vainly to intercede, demanding that southern Members be admitted. The clerk, his lesson well learned before, turned to Stevens and asked: "I wish to know when the matter of admitting southern Members will be taken up?"

With ill-concealed satisfaction, and with irony and malevolence in his every syllable, Old Thad Stevens pronounced the doom of a merciful and speedy Reconstruction. "I have no objections to answering that question," he said, with obvious relish. "I will press the matter at the proper time."

History records no clear picture of how those unhappy southerners felt or acted as they heard those fateful words and realized they were to be excluded. Crestfallen and humiliated, they left the floor, overcome with emotion. Behind them, "smiling" Schuyler Colfax, Speaker of the House, announced a quorum of 176 loyal Members present. A torrent of cheers burst forth when he cried out: "The duty of Congress is very clear—as clear even as the sun's pathway in the heavens—the door having been shut in the rebel faces, it is still to be kept bolted . . . until we can put them on such a basis of enduring justice as a guarantee every safeguard and protection to our loyal people."[131]

His wig rumpled and awry, Stevens lost no time in smashing over his attack the moment the House was organized and ready for business. He and his cohorts refused to permit the message from the President, always the first business of any session once the preliminaries were done with, to be read until his caucus resolution had been offered and passed. A Pennsylvania Conservative moved that it be held up until the President's message could be received, but the Radicals shouted him down. Nilblack, of Indiana, then moved that pending the question of admitting persons claiming seats in Congress, that such persons be entitled to the privilege of the floor. This, too, was gleefully voted down. The Stevens Resolution passed by a vote of 129 to

35. It created a Joint Select Committee of fifteen whose duties were to "Inquire into the condition of the so-called Confederate States and to report by bill if any were entitled to representation in Congress and until that time no Member is to be received in either House."[132]

Simultaneously, over on the Senate side, a similar motion was entered by Charles Sumner and swiftly passed. The Joint Committee sprang instantly into being: six Senators and nine Congressmen, with Thad Stevens as unofficial Chairman. The Senators were Fessenden, Howard, Harris, Grimes, Johnson, and Williams. The Representatives were Stevens, Washburne, Morrill, Grider, Bingham, Conkling, Boutwell, Blow, and Rogers.[133]

Through this political trickery, Stevens and Sumner had pocketed Congress and precipitated the most unusual political situation in American history. No bill or resolution relating to Southern affairs could be directly introduced in Congress. First it had to be referred to the Committee, there to be literally buried. Stevens probably invented the device early in November.

With lordly condescension, Congress now listened to President Johnson's first message to their body. That they were prepared to sneer and laugh was obvious. To their amazement and distress, they listened to a remarkable state paper.

Starting with a paean of thanksgiving that a merciful God had brought the Nation through a terrible period, Johnson skillfully summarized each and every issue confronting the country and begged careful, cautious consideration of them that the right way may be found for deliverance. He summed up his eight months' service with a digest of what he had done and tried to do. The South had carried out their part of the burden required of them, and now they were ready to reunite with the Union and bury the past.

He spoke of the position of the Negro and begged that Congress would abide by the Constitution and let the states work out their own problems without usurpation of rights. He stressed the economic state of the country and urged that preparations be made for a speedy recovery from the evils of an irredeemable currency before panics took place.

He wished public and private enterprise speedily to liquidate debts contracted in a paper currency and thus aid the return of a gold standard. There was shrewd comment on tariffs and taxation and a request that there be no favored classes and no special burdens on the poor. In closing he asked who would join with him in an effort to swiftly bring the Nation back to peace and prosperity.[134]

The Nation rocked with applause when they read and digested this message. Newspapers everywhere lauded the President for his amazing foresight, insight, and magnanimity. One editor went so far as to call him a demigod. From Europe came similar laudations and messages of congratulation. For almost a month, the White House was snowed under by letters and telegrams of praise.

It is well known today that George Bancroft, the noted historian, helped Johnson prepare this remarkable message. Before his death, he explained the extent of his work, the polishing of the draft prepared by Johnson. At the time his connection with the message became public, there was the usual hue and cry, but it swiftly died away. From Washington to Roosevelt the Second, there have been few, if any, men in that high office who have ever completely prepared their own messages.

Historians have frequently stated that the chief cause of the "war" between Congress and Andrew Johnson was the desire of the legislative body to recapture the rights lost to them during Lincoln's administration, when, as Commander in Chief, he necessarily and often bypassed them. Nothing, however, could be farthest from the truth, for Johnson himself, by his own conduct during the fight, proved that it was he and not the Congress who was desperately striving to maintain the constitutional system of checks and balances.

The cause of friction was the Radical effort completely to overthrow our regular form of government and substitute a parliamentary form, which would have made both the President and the Supreme Court subservient to Congress. The Radicals planned to centralize power by taking it away from the states and vesting everything in the hands of the legislative branch. Johnson was a "states' right man"

94

—an abider by the Constitution, and the Radicals' cry that the war and its aftermath had changed everything and that the government was now essentially different, caused him to fight them all the harder. Small wonder he compared himself with the Roman Tribune, who stood at the door of the Senate and cried out "Veto! Veto!" whenever he felt the people's rights were being infringed.

All during Johnson's administration, one finds a constant theft by Congress of the rights hitherto vested in the states, although these rights and the limitations of Congress are definitely outlined in the Constitution. But Old Thad Stevens had no more use or reverence for that document than he had mercy for a vanquished "rebel." He had no reverence for it because Thad Stevens was for "special privileges" and vested wealth, largely because they made his opinions profitable to him.

In every administration, there are usually one or two outstanding Members of Congress who are regarded as presidential spokesmen, and who also seek to gain executive approval of certain measures. In Johnson's administration, there was a conspicuous lack of such co-operation. What few meetings he did have with either Radicals or Moderates were marked by clashes, which was precisely what Stevens wanted. A large part of his maneuvers was to bait the President so characteristically he would see events in black and white and thus alienate the Moderates.[135]

In this connection, we find a resolution in the Journal of the Joint Committee of Fifteen, and presented to him by Moderates Fessenden, Reverdy Johnson, and Washburne. The desire was expressed to avoid all possible collision between the President and Congress in regard to their relative positions! The Committee thought it highly advisable that while Reconstruction was under consideration by the Committee, the President should take no further action unless it became imperatively necessary. Johnson answered this resolution with a cordial letter, indicating his desire for harmony and also urging haste in the work of the Committee. But harmony was not what Chairman Stevens desired,[136] and the President's temperamental disposition could be made a handy weapon.

95

The Radicals now swept on with their nefarious schemes to make Johnson impotent. On December 18, Stevens delivered a scathing speech in the House, in which he excoriated the President and declared the Radicals were against compromises of any sort. He also bluntly stated the coming fight was to be along party lines! There was a rebel-loving Democrat in the White House, he inveighed.

On January 8, 1866, the House passed a resolution seeking to take the command of troops in the conquered South out of the President's hands. In retaliation, Johnson instantly threatened to veto the bill giving suffrage to the Negroes of the District of Columbia. Stevens launched a vitriolic attack on the floor, calling Johnson "an alien enemy and a citizen of a foreign state who was not legally the President of the country!"[137]

That which incensed Johnson most was the refusal of Congress to seat the Representatives from his own state. Moderates sought desperately to bring this recognition about, but their hopes for an early victory were presently dashed to earth. The Freedman's Bill, authorized by Trumbull, of Illinois, a Democrat and a Moderate, proved the stumbling block.

To help "sell" the North and East on the idea of withholding recognition from the South, the rumor was deliberately passed that repudiation of the national debt and the dishonoring of war bonds was the first plan of southern Members. Naturally, banks and investors found great cause for alarm in this so-called scheme and were vigilant in backing up their Congressmen and in spreading the unbased rumor.

In passing the Freedman's Bill in February, 1866, first of their Reconstruction measures, Congress was easily and clearly unconstitutional and violating states' rights. Johnson readily conceded to Congress the right to legislate for the territories, but he rightly contended they had no authority over a sovereign state and its internal affairs. The South comprised states, not territories.

The first Freedman's Bureau Bill had been designed to help the recently freed slave. As the war ended, it came to embrace all of the South. Though there was some injustice to whites in the execution of its activities, for the most part it was reasonably fair. It sought to give the black a stake in society by assigning abandoned land to him, or seeking to lease or purchase farmland. It extolled work over idleness and that slothfulness was the mark of slavery. It acted as a court in Negroes' disputes. It tried to secure a just wage for the Negroes' labor and even extended its activities into upholding the sanctity of marriage. Some of the more moderate "black codes" drew on it.

Now the Radicals sought to perpetuate this measure. But the second bill was another matter. It attempted to broaden the Bureau's activities, thereby creating offices of patronage under Congress. And it set aside the state and federal civil courts in matters of disputes. It would have been all powerful.[138]

Johnson lost no time in vetoing the bill, returning it to Congress on February 19. The House was eagerly willing to pass it over the veto, but the Senate refused by a two-thirds vote to override Johnson.[139] The Moderates were jubilant and perhaps Johnson was likewise, for the Senate's action was cause for some hope. His veto, however, had cost him dearly, for the inducement had been held out to him that if he signed the bill, making it a law, Congress would recognize Tennessee. In anger Johnson refused the bribe. Three Cabinet members, Stanton, Harlan, and Speed, "regretted" his veto, but the President was eloquent and emphatic in his language of opposition.[140]

Thad Stevens, determined to have an issue between the Congress and President, with his cohorts, rushed through a rock-ribbed resolution denying representation to rebel states until both Houses would concur on the Freedman Bill. The Senate fell into line. Overnight the Nation seethed with argument—"What IS happening down there in Washington?" one citizen asked another.[141]

Some of the New York papers took up ready cudgels in Johnson's behalf. The *World* was especially kind, making the statement that Congress was really naught but a rump one, in that they sat without the eleven southern states and calmly sought to grind the South into the dust. But other newspapers, bought over by the Radicals, or else their

97

supporters, saw things in another light. They hailed with glee the fact that the Nation had a two-fisted Congress, able and willing to fight this traitor in the White House.

One thing was sure—Andrew Johnson still had enough friends who believed in him and thought his policies were right. They idolized him so much that they decided Washington's Birthday that year was an ideal time to stage a national party in his honor. All over the land that day there were rallies, old-fashioned picnics, bonfires, monster meetings, and similar affairs of the day. In churches, prayers were offered for his guidance, men and women hailed him and bewailed his rough treatment at the hands of the Radicals.

That day was probably the sunset of his national life, and, henceforth, he was doomed to go down, under the greatest barrage of insult, invective, libel, and lies ever directed against any man in American politics.

CHAPTER 13

THE TAILOR STANDS ALONE

Never before or since in American history has any public figure been obliged to suffer so much for his convictions as did Andrew Johnson. Soon from the very pulpits where only a few weeks before men of God had uttered fervent prayers for his protection and guidance, there came libelous thunder and despicable innuendoes assailing not only his patriotism, but his morals. The "great" Henry Ward Beecher, soon to face a jury for his relations with a young married woman of his parish (the scandal rocked the Nation), helped spread one of the most scurrilous of these, namely, that Senator Pomeroy, calling at the White House, found the President, his son, and son-in-law all too drunk to conduct business, "that the President kept a mistress at the White House...."[142]

Cornered by Johnson, both Beecher and Pomeroy made tardy disavowals and struggled to pass the "buck," but the mischief had been done and the wild tale overspread the country like a prairie fire. The tale of drunken orgies, livened by the presence of female pardon brokers, with whom Washington was filled, multiplied.

Fresh grist for the Radical propaganda mill came up from the South almost every day. Every time a white man was killed, a Negro hanged, or a woman raped, an effort was made to link the crime to the President's policy of leniency. It was inevitable that crime would be on the increase below the Mason-Dixon Line. A rigid social code, of white supremacy, was desperately trying to hold out until adjustments could be tested and made which would be fair to black and white alike.

The Committee of Fifteen was busily holding public sessions and "examining" witnesses of every description who would help to bear out their contention the South was not yet in a "fit" state to enjoy the blessings of reunion and the privilege of legislative representation. They threw the Schurz report to the Radical Press, ignoring Grant's observations. They continued to harp on the Black Codes. Johnson's veto of Freedman's Bureau Bill had closed hundreds of Negro schools, they alleged. Never before have such farcical hearings been conducted in Congress.

For five long months, solely for the purpose of delaying Presidential reconstruction, the Committee called before its members a parade of prejudiced witnesses, who gleefully condemned Johnson's policies and flayed the former slaveholders and Rebels for their present treatment of the wretched black. The charges and statements in 1866 made excellent campaign material.[143]

So long did the Committee delay taking up concrete plans for Reconstruction that Radical newspapers began to insist on action because they feared the Nation might clamor for Johnson's plan as better than none. To ease such feelings, the Committee brought forth several hazy proposals to amend the very constitution, but these came to naught. One proposal which would have based representation on population, provided the voting privilege was granted to persons of ALL COLOR, was brought out and swiftly passed by the House, only to be defeated by a narrow margin in the Senate. Finally, April 30, 1866, the Committee issued an eight-hundred-page report!

On Washington's Birthday, 1866, Johnson was serenaded before the White House by a tumultuous and cheering throng of admirers. They demanded a speech, and in a moment of thoughtlessness and against the advice of several Cabinet members who were present, Johnson launched forth in his best stump oratory. Before he knew it, someone in the crowd had brought up the subject of Congress and Johnson irrationally lashed out at Stevens and Sumner, calling them traitors who were seeking to destroy the Nation by their extreme measures. He also referred to Forney as a "dead duck." The crowd whooped and cheered approval. It was a terrible mistake and played into Stevens' hands. Schouler states that "Andrew Johnson's influence as Chief Executive and sectioned leader may be said to have culminated on that date." Until then he had the favor of the Nation. It had been impressed

100

with him and his moderation. His Cabinet was largely behind him—the double-dealing Stanton outnumbered. The Radicals had not moved, but were marking time.[144]

Meanwhile, the Moderates in the Senate upheld Johnson's veto of the Freedman's Bureau Bill; the Radicals attempted to capture control of that body. There had been an election contest over the seat of Senator Stockton, of New Jersey, a Johnson supporter. The Senate Judiciary Committee had heard the case and confirmed Stockton's rights to his seat. The Radicals contrived to bring the already closed matter back to the floor and through parliamentary sculduggery, Stockton was unseated. Johnson lost a friend and the Moderates lost a badly needed vote.

In March, the Radicals then moved to bring up the Civil Rights Bill. It was a bill the nature of which would cause furor in the twentieth, let alone the nineteenth, century. It sought to declare the Negro a citizen, which Seward considered laudable. But to the minds of Johnson and Welles, but not Stanton nor Harlan, the Bill contained many obnoxious features potently interfering with the constitutional rights of the states—"mischievous and subversive," as Welles put it. It tended toward centralization of power and would at the moment foment discord among the races. All the states, Johnson emphasized, were not now represented and thus could not consider so momentous a move—one which not only altered the constitution but affected the social mores of the people, referring specifically to marriages between the races. He vetoed it.[145]

One Cabinet member had hoped for his approval in order to reconcile the executive and congressional split and return the branches to a spirit of co-operation. Indeed, several Congressmen claimed that Johnson had led them to believe that he would sign it and they were bitter in their disappointed denunciation of him.[146]

With passions flaming high, the Senate overrode his veto by a vote of thirty-three to fifteen, one Senator being absent. Swiftly the House confirmed the Senate action.

This was the first congressional constitutional revolt of importance ever waged against a chief executive in American History, and it created a profound sensation among the legal profession and thoughtful citizens everywhere. They realized full well that the Radicals now had power and meant to use it, regardless of the Constitution and Supreme Court. The Democrats and Moderates in Congress were losing courage. To vote or even think counter to Radical politics meant political suicide.

About this time, Johnson began to take stock of the warnings from some of his faithful Cabinet members. Time and again, they had urged him not to make so many appointments to higher offices of men who were obviously Radical followers. In fact, despite their attitude towards him, the Radicals had never hesitated to demand patronage from the Chief Executive. For months, perhaps to win friends among, and therefore divide, Radical ranks, Johnson had given this patronage without hesitation. But these new officeholders had berated him almost from the first moment of appointment. In some spirit of well-deserved censor, Johnson now removed many of their traducers and finally reappointed those friendly to his policies. A great howl of rage went up from the Radical ranks. They called it an outrage that good men were being expelled because they adhered to their party! The idea for the Tenure-of-Office Act was thus given birth—the bill that would freeze into office all past appointees, forbidding the President to remove appointees without the permission of Congress. It was along about this time, too, that Johnson became seriously aware that his Cabinet would be better off, and likewise the Nation, if he were able to get rid of Stanton. Unfortunately, he merely thought about it. His old habit of procrastination was exerting itself.

In their efforts to increase control of the Congress, the Radicals now saw fit to create states of two of the territories, Colorado and Nebraska, having first made certain the new representatives would be fellows of their own stripe. Johnson promptly vetoed the bills. Congress would have overridden him, but Charles Sumner did a strange thing—he refused to side with his fellows because the new Colorado constitution contained the word "white" in describing her citizens! For once, perhaps, Sumner stuck to his guns about befriending the Negro. He voted against his pledges because they would not strike out that word, "white."

102

During the remainder of the session, Congress sent Johnson another Freedman's Bureau Bill and when he vetoed it, they passed it over his protest. His veto of the Nebraska Bill was secure, however, by means of the "pocket veto."[147]

Sometimes overlooked, but which evidences Radical schemes, was his veto of the New York and Montana Iron Mining and Manufacturing Bill, which would have made of this company a pre-emptor of public lands and accorded it a monopoly. Johnson told Congress, "the public domain is a national trust, set apart and held for the general welfare upon principles of equal justice, and not to be bestrewed as a special privilege upon a favored class."[148]

Driven to a frenzy by executive obstruction, Congress now passed a bill to admit Tennessee, but in the preamble they made it appear that Tennessee had accepted and agreed upon Radical reconstruction! If Johnson had signed it, he would be giving tacit approval of Radical plans. If he refused to sign it, he would be charged with having refused to admit his own state! Johnson refused to be caught by such a trick. On advice of a few friendly Senators, he signed the bill in a round-about-manner — approving of it in a message to Congress, which disregarded the Radical scheme. The Radicals protested the method as unconstitutional, but they were obliged to seat the Members from Tennessee.[149]

The first real effort at reconstruction on the part of the Committee of Fifteen was their drafting of the Fourteenth Amendment.[150] Stevens reported it to the House on April 30. It was an amendment largely meant to bolster the Civil Rights Bill and to reapportion Congressional representation on a basis of voting population. Johnson vetoed it; his veto was promptly overridden and the amendment was sent to the various states for ratification. Johnson was so furious he sent telegrams of protest to most of the governors, urging them not to ratify the amendment because it was infringement of states' rights. In presenting the amendment, Stevens had promised that if the southern states would adopt it, they would be given instant representation. Neither Johnson nor the South believed him—neither did anyone else with a grain of sense.[151]

Both Johnson and the conservative forces of the Nation were growing desperate at the everyday growth of power of the Radicals. The plight of the southern states had reached hideous depths. Race riots were becoming a constant menace and the slightest clash between the colors had endless woes behind it. As early as April 30, 1866, Memphis was swept by a race riot and before the affair was ended, forty-six Negroes had been killed. The Radicals promptly laid it at the door of the President. Truth is, he had been framed. Stanton had deliberately withheld from him an appeal for Federal troops to guard the area and prevent the riot from happening. Stanton held the appeal up for three days—until the riot was over, in fact. July 30, another terrible race riot came about in New Orleans, when Radical forces sought to force suffrage by calling a state-wide convention.

Governor Wells, of Louisiana, played a sorry role in the affair because of his irresolution. But State Attorney General Herron and Mayor Monroe, of New Orleans, did heroic work in trying to stave off the inevitable catastrophe. Both tried to contact General Sheridan, district military commander, but he proved to be away on a visit. General Baird, head of the local Freedman's Bureau, was second in command and he wired Stanton for instructions. With malice aforethought, Stanton held up the telegram for some eighteen days and Baird found himself in a terrible dilemma. On the other hand, General Herron and Mayor Monroe wired the President direct and he advised them he had instructed the military to sustain the local courts which had denied permission for the convention to be held. But Stanton, through whom he had issued the orders, failed to forward them. What happened next was red, raw tragedy.[152]

The convention met on the morning of July 30, but adjourned for lack of a quorum. That afternoon, a mob of armed, excited, and milling Negroes swept down on the hall. A white boy was shoved off the sidewalk and the police were called. Behind them came a huge crowd of white citizens, armed to the teeth. The Negroes fled inside the convention hall for shelter and, before long, shots were fired from the windows into the assembled crowd. The police, backed by the mob, stormed the building and a bloody massacre followed. Some two hundred Negroes were killed and many more were wounded. All over the city race rioting of fearful proportions broke out. The Federal troops finally appeared on the scene but the mischief had been done.[153]

The bloody affair had dire reactions on Johnson's fortunes. Thad Stevens and Charles Sumner bellowed out to the winds that the affair had been authored by none other than the President himself! Radical newspapers promptly took up the cudgels, charging Johnson with having aided and abetted in the affair, and they implied he was entirely responsible for it.

Naturally, the affair was a terrible blow to Johnson, for he found himself hemmed in on all sides by evil forces, who would neither fight fair nor in the open. One possibility seemed left to him—to take his fight directly to the people in the hope that in the coming fall Congressional elections they would break the Radical bloc against him. His faith in the people was the abiding passion of his life—they had trusted him; he had never failed them, and now he felt they would not betray or desert him, if only he could get the truth across.

That political campaign of 1866 is easily the most important one ever held in our country.[154] Had Johnson succeeded in breaking the Radical majority in either House or Senate, the whole history of our Nation would have been different and the unfortunate South would have been spared ten years of misery and tragedy. Nor would there be anything like the "Solid South" of today, with a great section of our country still "remembering" what should long ago have been forgotten. Johnson never had the opportunity to explain the issues to America, and for all his laudable efforts, he became the most pilloried and lampooned and libeled man in history.[155]

The importance of the campaign is evidenced by the fact that no less than four great political conventions were held that year for the sole purpose of either helping Johnson or else to tear him down. The first of these was the National Union Convention, held in Philadelphia on August 14. Ten thousand cheering Johnson sympathizers met to do what they could to save his political fortunes. How confident Johnson was that success would crown the affair is indicated by a telegram to the Postmaster General and to his Secretaries, Browning and Randall, who attended as his Representatives: "The finger of Providence is unerring and will guide you

105

safely through. The people must be trusted and the country will be restored."[156]

This convention marked the first great reunion of men who had fought against each other in the late war. Many had been friends earlier in life; then torn apart by the strife, and now reunited in a common cause. It was a tremendous event and would have had far-reaching effects throughout the country had it only been fairly reported. But not so! The Radical press quickly "sold" the country that those scenes of unity were additional proof that Andy was arm-in-arm with the late traitors who had drenched the land in blood. Thomas Nast's cartoons and Petroleum Nasby's vulgar quips shattered every laudable action the convention brought about.

Behind the Philadelphia convention was the scheme of Assistant Postmaster General A. W. Randall. Built on the framework of the old National Union Party, it was a conclave of old Whigs, the disrupted Democratic party, and the conservative Republicans. Randall planned it as a forerunner of a national speaking tour by the President, but the Radicals swiftly and easily wrecked the scheme's effectiveness. A legitimate convention, in which delegates had been duly elected from each of the thirty-six states, it nevertheless smacked too much of Copperheadism and Secession for the Nation to freely accept. One telling argument against the affair was the fact that the majority of the delegates from the deep South came attired in their old Confederate uniforms. Truth is, most southerners either had to wear their old army garb or adopt barrels. They were actually destitute of clothing! The cartoonists didn't explain this tragic lack of raiment.

Johnson's speech of "acceptance" of the report of the Convention is one of the most touching perorations of his whole career. He declared he had taken his stand upon the broad principles of liberty and the Constitution and there "is not power enough on earth to drive me from it." He pointed out that had he merely wished power, he might easily have acquired enough to make himself dictator of all America by merely having signed the Freedman's Bureau Bill and the Civil Rights Bill. With fifty millions in cash provided by the Freedman's Bill and an army at his heels, he could have tied up the Nation to his own purposes. "But, gentlemen! My pride and my ambition have been to occupy that position which retains all power in the hands of the people!"

Perhaps we should briefly cut back here and explain that early in July three of the Cabinet members, unwilling to go counter to the Radical policies, had resigned—Dennison, Harlan, and Speed. Johnson was mistaken in not picking friendly Democrats as their successors, replacing them with Randall, of Wisconsin, Browning, of Kentucky, and Stanbery, of Ohio. At this same time, he was urgently begged by countless friends to demand the resignation of Stanton whose actions openly reeked of treachery. It has since been explained that Johnson refused because as a southern Democrat he was under too much suspicion and he felt his choice of Republican Cabinet members would help make him more acceptable to the country. Alas for such reasoning!

August 28, with a great fanfare, began the sorry event known as the "Swing around the Circle"[157]—the President's personal appeal to the Nation. His retinue was an amazing one—Secretaries Seward, Randall, and Welles, General Grant, Admiral Farragut, and some fifty others, including the President's daughter, Mrs. Patterson, Mrs. Welles, and Mrs. Grant. Welles, in his diary, called the affair a "pageant" and it certainly started out with such an air.[158] The return trip to the Capital, however, might have well been likened to a cortegé, for what had been meant as a happy, harmonious event soon took on the air of a funeral.

Baltimore, the first stop along the long route, gave the party an impressive reception. A crowd estimated at more than one hundred thousand lined the streets and struggled to hear the speeches. Cannon roared and bands revived stirring music. The President was almost mobbed by hand-shakers. On then to Philadelphia, where similar scenes were enacted. The ovation in New York was almost enough to turn any man's head—a half-million people paid a fervent, frenzied tribute. Stirring indeed were the

107

lines from Johnson's great speech at the banquet held at Delmonico's in his honor—"Let there be common feeling—our country first, our country last, our country all the time—disregarding party for the public good!"

The Radicals grew worried as they observed the tremendous ovations being accorded the one man who stood between them and their ambitions. All too well they saw that Johnson was right in his claim that if he could only tell his story to the people, they would believe and back him. So, they devised pitfalls from which Johnson could manage no escape. Well did they know his background and his terrible temper when pressed too closely. Cunningly they schemed to take advantage of his failings —especially that tendency of his to offer "Tennessee stumping,"[159] in which he had great confidence.

The Radical method was so simple it is surprising that Johnson allowed himself to be trapped. They packed his meetings with plug-uglies and roisterers, who were ordered to interrupt his speeches whenever possible. Apprehensive of this very possibility, Johnson's closest friends had begged him to exercise great caution in his addresses and never to allow himself to be drawn into arguments from the platform. Senator Doolittle, of Wisconsin, was especially insistent in expressing himself. "Do not allow yourself to be drawn into extemporaneous speeches in the excitement of the moment! You are being followed by the reporters of a hundred presses, who may do nothing but misrepresent. Say nothing which has not been carefully prepared," he advised while the trip was in progress. "Enemies have never been able to get any advantage from anything you ever wrote. But what you have said extemporaneously has given them a handle to use against you."

The debacle began when the party arrived in Cleveland.[160] An enormous crowd gathered before his hotel and shouted for him to appear. Planning merely to show himself and bow to what he thought was their courtesy, the President appeared on a balcony. Hecklers swiftly goaded him into a situation from which there was no escape. A cry of "Hang Jeff Davis! Hang Thad Stevens!" proved the fuse that swept him off into one of his "stump" speeches that the Radical papers informed the Nation the next day was "the most disgraceful ever delivered by any President of the United States!"

Four days after the affair, it was learned that the outrage had been arranged from Washington and that thirty or forty hecklers had been paid from funds sent by the Union League Club. In Chicago, a few days later, a similar outrage took place. Emboldened by their success in Ohio, the Radicals added other embellishments. Men paraded the streets bearing banners reading "NO Welcome to Traitors!" and bands played the "Dead March," from Saul.

In St. Louis, just before a great civic banquet, Johnson was trapped again, and this time the affair became almost a riot. As a matter of fact, the Swing around the Circle did result in a few deaths and more than one cracked skull, as various factions fought back and forth. A factor in these street fights was the ill-fated Fenian invasion of Canada early in the summer. Eight hundred armed Irishmen had marched across the Niagara River and seized Fort Erie in a mad scheme to force England to grant freedom to Ireland. The Radicals promptly used the event to cut the Irish vote from Johnson.

In the Johnson party were scores of newspapermen,[161] mostly unfriendly, and their stories of the trip mark a new high in political slander. From Cleveland on, they constantly reported the President was on a drunken orgy, as were likewise the other members of his party. Only one man in his party came under this status, and that was the unfortunate General Grant. Intoxication forced him to leave the party at Cleveland and again at St. Louis, his condition forcing him to retreat from the eyes of the public.[162]

On September 15, Johnson and the majority of his party, saddened and reflective, returned to Washington. Although a great parade and a welcome had been arranged in his honor and the affair went off with never a hitch, Johnson knew in his heart that his mission had failed[163] and that, for the time being, the Constitution and all that it stood for was in the hands of the Nation's enemies. He was sad, thoughtful, and deeply chagrined, but he was too much of a fighter to cry quits.

One things was sure—at the White House, patiently waiting for him, was one person at least who had never ceased to believe in him: bedridden Eliza.

The last strains of his escort band were still echoing up from the Avenue as he hastened up the stairs to her room. Now in his tragic hour of despair, he tumbled to the side of her bed, groping with shaking fingers for her own calming clasp.

CHAPTER 14

THE PRESIDENT ON TRIAL

A jubilant, power-mad Congress assembled in December, 1866. They considered their success in the recent elections as an endorsement of the people's will and a repudiation of all that Johnson struggled for. "King Andy" was dead, or else surely dying.

If they expected a belligerent message from Johnson, they quickly found themselves mistaken. Instead, the Tailor sent them a dignified paper that must have shamed many of them because of the logic of his stand. He reviewed the present state of the Nation—that although peace was now a matter of fact, more than one-fourth of the states remained without representation in Congress, as was their legal right. Some seventy duly accredited Senators and Representatives were being unlawfully deprived of their states and the whole Nation would suffer until admission was accorded them. It was a lengthy, able review of the actual facts, but the Radicals now had the bit in their teeth and they manifested their reaction with jeers.

Stevens launched the opening attack upon the President. On December 13, 1866, he introduced a bill abolishing the "Johnson" government of North Carolina and providing for a new scheme of Reconstruction. With brazen effrontery, Stevens told the House the elections were his authority to inflict VENGEANCE ON THE SOUTH and that he intended to carry it out, regardless of what the Nation suffered from his sowing of the whirlwind!

Prior to his introduction of this amazing and disturbing bill, another of Stevens' pet measures to hamstring and shore the President of authority had been slipped over: his colleagues eagerly repealed an Act of 1862 which permitted the President to proclaim amnesty to those who had taken part in Secession. Hard on the heels of this measure,

111

they enacted a statute maintaining continuous sessions of Congress, the purpose of which, as they boldly exclaimed, was to maintain a constant guard on the treasonous attitude of the President!

In the Senate, Charles Sumner was feverishly pressing for immediate consideration of his bill to permit Negroes to vote in the District of Columbia. Election officers who failed to accept their votes were liable to a fine of five thousand dollars or a year's imprisonment, or both. His arguments were naive and frank. "Once you needed the muskets of the colored man; now you need their votes," his unctuous voice rang out. Swiftly his fellows passed the measure and the House quickly concurred. Johnson promptly vetoed it, but Sumner urged his willing colleagues to override the Tailor's objections and they did so with scarcely a negative vote. It is worth noting here that the citizens of Washington had already rejected a scheme of this sort by an overwhelming vote. After eight years of Radical sculduggery in connection with this statute, Congress repealed the measure in 1874 and gave the District a commission form of government.

Although they already controlled both Houses, the Radicals now sought to swell their ranks by according statehood to Colorado and Nebraska, in which territories they had already been assured of "proper" representation. The stunt had been tried the prior year, but Johnson had vetoed their efforts. In their new bills, the Radicals inserted Negro suffrage clauses. Johnson vetoed the measures, contending in the case of Colorado that its population of thirty thousand was insufficient under the Constitution. He was sustained in this veto, but Nebraska was brought into the Union over his objection.

In the latter part of January and the forepart of February, several of Johnson's most sincere friends begged him to change his entire Cabinet in a final effort to clarify the situation with Congress. Johnson, according to Colonel Moore, his Secretary, admitted that such a change would settle his troubles within two hours. However, he saw no way in which to do so without hurting Cabinet members, whose friendship he valued.

On February 6, Stevens introduced his infamous bill to "wipe out the pretended state governments of Virginia, North and South Carolina, Georgia, Florida, Alabama, Louisiana, Mississippi, Texas, and Arkansas, and place them under military rule as conquered territories!" It was a terrible blow against the South, and although the President had expected the measure, the implications and possibilities were nothing less than ominous. All that he had fought for was now to be wiped out and greater suffering than ever was to be the lot of the unhappy late Confederacy.

Brooking not a whisper of questioning, the Pennsylvanian held his followers spellbound as he read his bill and gloated over what he assured his rapt audience the measure would result in. He proposed the conquered states be divided into five military districts, each to be "ruled" by at least a Brigadier General, who would be granted almost unlimited powers. These officers would be given rights to dismiss governors now in office, prevent elections, suspend the functioning of all courts, and other despotic powers, for which they were to be accountable solely to Congress.

Although the President has always been recognized as Commander in Chief of the Army, as provided by the Constitution, Stevens' bill provided these military rulers would be appointed by the "General of the Army," namely, Grant, who was already aligning himself with the Radicals and grooming himself as Johnson's successor. It should be mentioned here that at the request of Secretary Stanton, Boutwell, of Massachusetts, had, as early as December, added an amendment to the Army Appropriation bill, requiring that all orders to the army which Johnson might issue would have to be first given to the Secretary or the Commanding General. Stanton had informed Boutwell that the President had formed the habit of issuing his own orders directly and that there was grave danger he was up to serious mischief. Thus, this special provision in the new Reconstruction bill was another slap at the President.

The House didn't waste time debating the measure, but, nevertheless, the record shows that fifty-five men were honest enough to vote No! The trouble was, there were twice as many Radicals on hand to jam it through. Men said

113

of Thad Stevens that day that he never seemed younger, happier, nor in finer fettle. Audaciously, he had spoken of himself and his cohorts as Gods from on high. His power over lesser men had intoxicated him worse than alcohol ever had—now out of a certainty, he would get revenge for what raiding southern troops had done to his little iron foundry during the war!

His enthusiasm met an instant rebuff in the Senate, however. Of fellow-villains there, he had a plenty, but there still remained a stalwart minority whose sense of fair play and righteousness could not accept his plan verbatim. Senators Cowan and Doolittle were still siding with the Tailor and their voices rose in instant opposition. Democratic allies went promptly to their aid when Senator Saulsbury, of Delaware, cried out aghast that he "would not touch, taste nor handle the unclean thing." Other Democrats felt the same way, McDougall, of California, tearing the bill apart with savage thrusts.

With Sumner ranting and raving for passage, and Democratic and Conservative Senators fiercely picking the measure to pieces, Senator Sherman stepped into the breach with a slightly less painful substitute, less offensive in its phraseology, and including a way whereby the southern states could emancipate themselves from the horrors of continuous military rule. His substitute placed appointment of the military commanders in the President's hands. Any state wishing to return to the Union would have to pass the Fourteenth Amendment; draft a constitution in a state convention, whose delegates were to be elected by ALL citizens, regardless of color. The final constitution was then to be adopted by an electorate selected under the new state constitution. Then it must be sent to Congress for examination. If Congress accepted it, then the state would be allowed to re-enter the Union after her duly elected representatives had taken an ironclad oath of allegiance.

Charles Sumner was so enraged at these changes that he fled from the Senate, refusing to vote. He threw another tantrum when, led by Stevens, the House refused to concur with the Senate, whereupon the Senate, suddenly stubborn, denied the lower House a conference. For a week there was ire and tension between the two bodies, then Stevens, realizing that the legislative term was drawing to a close, reluctantly accepted the Senate's substitute measure, first however, demanding (and getting) several odious amendments which added to the woes of the despairing South.

The final measure, entitled an "Act to Provide for the More Efficient Government of the Rebel States," passed both Houses on the 22nd of February and was hurriedly sent to the President. Four days before, there had preceded it another legislative blow at the President and his powers —the infamous Tenure-of-Office Act.

In the Swing around the Circle, Johnson had frightened more than one of the Radicals with an oft-repeated threat to remove certain Federal employees whose disloyalty not only rankled him, but numerous voters as well. He never was specific as to who was getting the official boot, nor did he ever get a chance to exert it. For, apprehensive of what he might do, Stanton and others decided to tie his hands in making dismissals. They framed a bill freezing into office all such appointees which were confirmed by the Senate. Thus, the President was to be shorn of his powers to remove an appointee unless the Senate approved his action. Stanton outlined the first draft of this bill, and his reason for doing so was his knowledge that Johnson had at last become aware of his treachery and was planning his dismissal.

The Tenure-of-Office Act withstood days of debate and more than one change before its final passage. One of the leading objections to it was its obvious unfairness to the Executive in the selection and retaining of his Cabinet, even some of the most rabid of the Radicals, realizing how necessary it was for harmony's sake, that a Chief Executive be given some say over his advisors. They weren't so concerned over harmony in Andy Johnson's Cabinet as they were afraid of establishing a precedent, when a Radical might inherit the office.

In their desperate debate for words and phrases that might enshackle the President and prevent him from ousting the wretched, conniving Stanton, the Senate unwittingly provided the very loophole by which Johnson was later to remove him from office. This came about as a result of a House conference over the measure—the Senate refusing to accept the demand of the lower body that the Cabinet be tied up as all other presidential appointees. Finally, in a tired moment, the House Members felt that they had won a victory when they agreed to the clause: "Members of the Cabinet shall hold their offices respectively for and during the term of the President by whom they may have been appointed, and for one month thereafter, subject to removal by and with the advice and consent of the Senate."

The Radicals had forgotten that Johnson had retained all of Lincoln's Cabinet and that therefore, by their very words, he was not bound to continue retaining them longer than one month after his succession to office! Unaware of this for the time being, the House had a mild celebration—jubilantly feeling they had won a smashing victory over the fool in the White House, who still believed in the inviolability of the Constitution.

Johnson laid both the Reconstruction measure and the Tenure-of-Office Act before his Cabinet on the same day for their decision. The Reconstruction Act was objectionable to them all save Stanton, and he promptly urged the President to sign it. But sign it, the Tailor would not. To Colonel Moore, his Secretary, hurrying in and out of the room, Johnson exclaimed angrily, "I would sooner sever my right arm from my body than deprive any citizen of the right of habeas corpus!" The President decided to veto the measure, but determined to make his message thereon more to the Nation at large than to Congress, for he felt a great issue was at stake. With this in view, he asked Jeremiah Sullivan Black to come to the White House and give him a hand.

Although history holds him up as the author of the original Tenure-of-Office bill, Stanton's reactions to the bill when it was brought up for discussion in the Cabinet meeting almost stagger belief. While the other Members condemned it openly, none was so plain-spoken and vehement as the little wine-muddled deceiver. Welles records him as crying out that "No man of proper sense of honor

116

would remain in the Cabinet when invited to resign!" Whereupon, the Tailor broadly hinted before everyone present that his resignation would be acceptable to him!

Stanton may have suffered terrible pangs at that moment, but he made no sign that he had heard the President speak. Several other hints went by unnoticed and then Johnson demanded that he write the veto message for him because other matters kept him from doing so.

The Secretary of War managed to find his tongue and his excuse, "I cannot do so because of rheumatism in my arm!" Johnson then turned to Seward and requested him to handle the matter. Seward agreed, on the proviso that Stanton give him a hand. The War Secretary may not have liked the task, but before he realized it, he found himself saddled with the task of vetoing his own pet project, and when Johnson sent both measures back bearing his disapproval on March 2, Stanton had written what is still conceded a masterfully done message of objection.

Between them, Johnson and Jeremiah Black devised a veto objection to the Military Reconstruction Act that was almost twenty thousand words long, not only addressed to Congress, but also to the Nation. Johnson wanted everybody to know why he, for one, refused to sit back and, as Chief Executive, administer a law which was not only criminally unfair to fellow Americans, but downright unconstitutional. His arguments are lucid, forceful, and plain enough for any schoolboy to understand today, yet he might as well have given them to apes to peruse as the followers of Stevens and Sumner.[164]

That body received his castigation in mock silence and disdain. Swiftly they repassed both measures over his objections and then settled back to enjoy the spectacle of both a man and a vast section trying desperately to cope with a situation that was worse than King Canute struggling against the incoming tides.

Impeachment is one of the most awkward words in the English language, for it seems to imply conviction for odious reasons, whereas in reality, it merely refers to the method employed in bringing political charges of malfeasance against a public official. It never indicates guilt, but such is the mental make-up of people that to countless thousands whose knowledge of history is sketchy, Johnson is only remembered by some such statement as "Let me see, wasn't he the President who was impeached?"

In a strict interpretation of words, we must confess then that Andrew Johnson was impeached, but because the charges against him were untrue, he was found not guilty. His reputation, however, will always suffer as long as man lives, because men will largely remember he was brought to trial, and, therefore, there must have been some reason or other for the action.

His chief persecutor was a grafter. As one-time Canal Commissioner of Pennsylvania, Stevens quickly moved himself into a position where he could not have withstood public audit of his books. His enemies said he used public money to advance his party, and, of course, that meant himself. In debt thirty thousand dollars when he entered Congress, he boasted of having paid this off within ten years, albeit he lived high, gambled inordinately, and outwardly drew only a Congressman's salary of thirty-six hundred dollars per year. Ten years later, when he died, he left a small fortune.

In the Johnson papers, there is a brief memorandum, written in pencil by Johnson. It is the record of a holiday excursion taken by himself and Secretary Seward the afternoon of September 6, 1868, months after the abortive Impeachment trial.

On the 6th Sept. Sunday, 1868, Mr. Seward and myself rode out some seven or eight miles on the road leading to Malsboro, Md.—near place called old fields, we drove out into a shade grove of oak trees—While there taking some refreshment, in the current of conversation on various subjects, the Secretary asked the question if it had ever occurred to me how few Members there were in Congress whose actions were entirely above and beyond pecuniary influence. I replied that I had never attempted to reduce it to an accurate calculation, but regretted to confess that there was a much smaller number exempt than at one period of life I had supposed them to be—He then stated you remember that the appropriation of the seven $ million for the payment of Alaska to the Russian Govnt was hung up or brought to a deadlock in the H of

118

Reps—While the appropriation was thus delayed the Russian minister stated to me that John W. Forney stated to him that he needed $30,000 that he had lost $40,000, by a faithless friend and that he wanted the $40,000 in gold—That there was no chance of the appropriation passing the House of Reps without certain influence was brought to bear in its favor— The $30,000 was paid hence the advocacy of the appropration in the Chronicele—He also stated that $20,000 was paid to R. J. Walker and F. P. Stanton for their services—N. P. Banks chairman of the committee on foreign relations $8,000 and that the incorruptible Thaddeus Stevens received as his "sop" the moderate sum of $10,000—All these sums were paid by the Russian minister directly and indirectly to the respective parties to secure appropriation money the Govnt had stipulated to pay the Russian Govnt in solemn treaty which had been ratified by both Govnts.—Banks and Stevens was understood to be the counsel for a claim against the Russian Govnt for Arms which had been furnished by some of our citizens— known as the Perkins Claim—Hence a fee for their influence in favor of the appropriation Etc.—Banks was chairman of the Committee on foreign relations—[165]

In this connection, of the seven million, two hundred thousand dollars paid to Russia for Alaska, a report from London, through whose financial center the final draft was passed, showed that the sum forwarded to Russia was but five million dollars! How many others of that period got their "share" of the other two million and two hundred thousand dollars![166]

When the Library of Congress acquired the private papers of President Johnson, there was among the scores of boxes a fat little shorthand notebook, once the property of Colonel W. G. Moore, one of the President's secretaries. The Library transcribed Moore's notes and under date of March 10, 1868, Johnson dictated "Four of the men selected to prosecute me would have made a half-million, apiece on the Alta Vela deal had I okeyed it!"

Who were the four men selected finally as prosecutors of Johnson during the Impeachment trial? They were Thaddeus Stevens, the noble "Old Commoner," Senator Logan, Senator Ben Butler, and Representatives James A. Garfield, James G. Blaine, John A. Bingham, J. K. Moorehead, and W. K. Koontz; these are names that Johnson read off that day to his Secretary as interested more than a little in his decision in the Alta Vela matter.

Alta Vela was a little sea-bird rookery off the coast of Santo Domingo in the Caribbean Sea. Rich in guano deposits, it had long been a bone of contention between a Baltimore fertilizer concern and the Central American Republic, then in the throes of internal revolt. Patterson, Murguindo and Company, of Baltimore, claimed title and all rights to the invaluable phosphates. Dispossessed by Santo Domingo, they stormed into Washington and retained Jeremiah Sullivan Black as their counsel. They induced Black to approach various Senators and Representatives in their behalf and, finally, the State Department was asked to intervene in favor of the American claimants.

In weighing the factors developing into the Impeachment trial, one is constantly struck by the fact that Stevens, from the very start of his battle with Johnson, counseled his more hasty-minded colleagues "Not yet!" when they cried out for impeachment. He regarded it as the final and greatest weapon in his armory and he meant to use it only as a last resort. As master mind of the Hill and chief juggler of the political marionettes, he was timing things for personal reasons.

Often hinted on the floor, it was not until December 17, 1866, that the first resolution demanding Johnson's impeachment was made. The introducer was James M. Ashley, of Toledo, described by writers of his day as a fanatic and mildly insane. Devoid of all decency and fairness, Ashley launched into a crazy diatribe, in which he accused Johnson of everything, including murder. His resolution failed to win the necessary two-thirds majority. The Milligan case, denying the right of Congress to suspend civil trial by jury anywhere a court was functioning, was a blow to Radical plans, as far as the South went, and they were greatly alarmed by the Court's statement that the Constitution of the United States could not be suspended nor martial law exist where courts are open. It was this setback that had prompted Ashley's resolution.

On January 24, 1867, another scatterbrained Radical,

Benjamin Loan, of Missouri, brazenly charged Johnson with the murder of Lincoln and introduced a resolution calling for a complete investigation. It swiftly passed and was turned over to the Judiciary Committee for handling. Promptly the Members set eagerly to work on their amazing quest—the search for links which might establish a tie between Booth and Andrew Johnson![167]

At great public cost, Ashley and several other Members, aided by Ben Butler, Sumner, and Wade, combed the whole land in a fruitless search for "documents and men" rumored to reveal all and know everything linking the Tailor to the higher-ups behind the assassination of Lincoln. Ashley visited jails and consorted with the vilest criminals, openly offering to buy at highest prices evidence, real or manufactured! One of those he thus approached was Sanford Conover, alias Dunham. Conover, then languishing in Capitol Prison, while awaiting transfer to a Federal Penitentiary, had been sentenced to ten years for his part in furnishing perjured testimony to Secretary Stanton in the Cabinet officer's great effort to link Jefferson Davis with the murder of Lincoln. His testimony was so obviously fraudulent that both judge and jury recoiled in amazement. That Stanton and others knew it to be false, there is no doubt, for they paid Conover and several of his accomplices more than eleven hundred dollars from Department of Justice funds![168]

Ashley made a number of visits to Conover and brazenly offered to buy testimony that would hold up in court, linking Johnson to Booth, and thus, accessory to Lincoln's assassination. Or, he was ready to buy any other kind of "evidence" that might show up Johnson as a traitor to the Nation. Conover was more than willing to oblige, offering to procure letters and witnesses, but in return he not only wanted a fat check, but a presidential pardon as well!

Believe this or not, but Ben Butler and other Radical Senators had the audacity to ask Johnson for such a pardon, knowing full well that the benefactor of Johnson's clemency would then turn around and falsely betray him! It happened, however, that the President was ahead of them. Dr. William Duhamel, prison physician, was a personal friend. Learning from a cell mate of Conover what was in the wind, he wrote the President of the plot against him. The deal quickly fell through and, with never a qualm, Conover, endeavoring to gain presidential favor for himself, wrote a full confession of what the Radicals had tried to get him to do and had it conveyed to Johnson.[169]

Unswerved by failure in his diabolical machinations, Ashley now turned to another prisoner, none less than John H. Surratt, whose unfortunate mother had died on the gallows as an accomplice of Booth. Surratt had fled the country after Lincoln's assassination, making his way to Italy, and thence escaping to Egypt, where he was finally captured. A U. S. gunboat had but recently brought him back, and now he was in another cell in the same prison with Conover. Through one Rev. W. B. Matchett, Ashley offered Surratt a chance to save his neck and at the same time remove the stigma from his dead mother's name, by agreeing to name Johnson as a party to the Lincoln plot. It is to Surratt's great credit that he not only indignantly refused, but so did his sister, Anne.

Spurred on by Ben Butler, and harried by Loan and Ashley, committee investigators flocked all over the Capitol, and even across the state of Tennessee, trying vainly to pin something on the President. Apparently, it couldn't be done! Even his bank accounts and cancelled checks were dragged before the committee and searched with microscopic care for some link with Booth or other suspect. But to their insane prayers came no answers.[170]

There came a day when Ashley had to admit both to himself and others that Justice wasn't as blind as he thought her to be. Search and connive as best he could, he hadn't been able to find a single iota to back up his claims and those of the psychopathic Loan. Angry and indignant Democratic members of the Judiciary Committee summoned him to the witness stand and demanded to know what he meant by his wild charges against the President; furthermore, where was this promised evidence for which so much good money had already been expended.

Hemming and hawing nervously, and finding his composure badly ruffled, Ashley struggled to find words. When

122

they did come, any listening psychiatrist would have speedily certified him as insane, but his colleagues evidently didn't feel he was exactly a menace to the Nation, although they themselves were angry.

> I have not yet presented my evidence because it is not legal evidence, naively asserted the Ohioan, and therefore, it would not satisfy the great mass of men who do not concur with me in my theory about this matter! What was his theory? demanded the Committee. Ah, I have always believed that President Harrison and President Taylor and President Buchanan were poisoned for the express purpose of putting the Vice Presidents in the Presidential office . . . when Mr. Lincoln was assassinated, from my standpoint, I could come to a conclusion which impartial men, holding different views, could not come to. It would not amount to legal evidence.

The Committee dismissed the witness in indignation and disgust. Ashley seems not to have realized he had admitted he was not impartial in the matter! The Committee was obliged to state that "owing to the magnitude of the task, they were unable to bring in a report," and would the House and Senate continue their existence so they might accomplish something? But the country was convinced of Ashley's distortions[171] and thought the matter closed, but the Radicals could not allow the situation to rest.

On the 8th day of March, 1867, during the opening days of the new 40th Congress, Ashley got the floor on a matter of personal privilege. He used that privilege to utter the worst vituperative speech ever made against an American President on the floor of either House of Congress. In fact, his language became so vile that even Speaker Colfax, infamous Radical himself, had to call him to order.[172]

The next day, Andrew Johnson found some strange consolation in his mail. There was a personal letter from Frank Smith, a banker friend of his in New York, asserting that to HIS KNOWLEDGE ASHLEY HAD RECEIVED FIFTY THOUSAND DOLLARS IN GOLD from a group of New York speculators for trumping up impeachment charges, their purpose being to manipulate the gold market![173] Remember that Johnson had already informed the Nation earlier in his administration that their next struggle would be against vested wealth. Now that trouble was coming with speed. By the time Grant became President, the gold speculators were to have their day.

During the year 1867, there were six attempts to impeach Johnson and all of them failed to win the necessary votes, despite no end of chicanery, bribery, and struggles. So bitter did the struggle become that men forgot themselves in moments of acid debate and, as a result of one of these "forgetful" moments, Andrew Johnson learned a dreadful thing he had been unaware of before.

He learned that Secretary Stanton and Judge Holt had tricked him into signing the death warrant for Mrs. Surratt without permitting him to see the military court's recommendation for mercy!

The story leaked out in a curious way. Senator Bingham, who had been a leading member of the military court, and now a Senator from Ohio, was pressing home a bill to aid destitute whites in the South. Something he said offended the testy Ben Butler and the two men exchanged hot, bitter words. The frog-eyed "Hero of Fort Fisher" [sic] retaliated with the statement: "The only victim of this gentleman's prowess that I know of was an innocent woman hung upon the scaffold; one Mrs. Surratt. And I can sustain the memory of Fort Fisher if he and his present associates can sustain him in shedding the blood of a woman tried by a military commission and convicted without sufficient evidence, in my judgment!"[174]

Stunned, Bingham struggled to defend himself, but the enraged ex-General had the bit between his teeth. In a few moments, he was spilling out the story of the diary found on Booth's body and it had been withheld from the court and someone in government had deliberately torn pages from it.

Andrew Johnson heard these things with anger in his heart. Quietly he investigated his relations with Secretary Stanton, however, becoming strained and icy-formal. On August 5, 1867, John Surratt, son of Mary Surratt, was placed on trial as an accomplice in the murder of Lincoln. His lawyer, taking advantage of what had been divulged on the floor of the Senate, dared the government to introduce

124

Booth's diary in court. Judge Bingham, again acting for the prosecution, waved the diary and what he claimed had been the court's plea for mercy from Mrs. Surratt, and which they had vainly submitted to the President![175]

Johnson was astounded. Scarcely had the charges and countercharges ceased to echo in the courtroom but his friends apprised him of things. He called Colonel Moore, his secretary, to him and dictated a curt note, ordering Stanton to resign his office for the good of the country! Johnson was never so angry. How dared Stanton say he had been handed an appeal from the court, asking for mercy for Mrs. Surratt?

That very day, Johnson appointed General Grant to succeed Stanton as Secretary of War.[176] Grant accepted. The appointment was in bad judgment. Previously, Grant had wavered much between Johnson and the Radicals. He served until January 14, 1868, when he quit the job with never a formal notice to the President. All he did was lock his office door and turn the keys over to his assistant. Grant's final action had ended months of disagreement with the President, especially with Johnson's desire to remove the district commanders in the South. Johnson demanded an inquiry and, before presidential supporters, he quizzed the General unmercifully and without tact, causing Grant to stammer explanations. Johnson branded him a conspirator with the Radicals.[177] Grant so infuriated Johnson that he became his lifelong enemy, and there was no love lost.

There was much furor over Johnson's removal of Stanton. On December 12, 1867, as required by the words of the Tenure-of-Office Act, Johnson sent a message to the Senate, informing them he had removed Stanton and had appointed Grant. Of course, the transaction had taken place four months before, but Congress had been in adjournment and unable to take any official action. However, those four months had been a period of violent debate all over the Nation as men argued and fought over the President's action. The Radicals were especially excited over the affair. They had come upon their prime cause to impeach their hated enemy.

At the same time Johnson sent his message to the Senate,

the ex-secretary filed a statement of his own, charging that he had been wrongfully removed from office without the approval or consent of Congress. On January 13, 1868, the matter came up on the floor of the House and in great uproar that body voted that the President had acted without authority and was in contempt of Congress.

Johnson was angered beyond words at the infringement of his constitutional rights to choose his own official family. The Cabinet agreed with him in his proposal that the war secretaryship be now offered to General Sherman. But Sherman declined, and on February 21, Adjutant General Lorenzo Thomas was given the appointment and, because of the legal question raised by the Tenure-of-Office Act, it was specified that the President was "acting under authority of the Act of 1789," at which time the office was first created.[178]

Briefly, after Grant turned the key in his door and tossed it to his secretary and then fled in search of some badly needed stimulant, who should come into the building but the discredited Stanton, fortified with wine, a basket of provisions, and flanked by determined Radical Members of Congress! Using the key he had never turned in, Stanton entered his old office and placed himself in a state of siege! He posted bewildered armed guards at the door and brazenly informed the clerks that he was there to stay by authority of Congress![179]

In the White House, Johnson, learning of the startling news, wrote a curt letter of dismissal and sent it over by messenger. He called General Thomas in, gave him his new appointment and ordered him to go oust Stanton and proceed with his new duties! A debonair, easy-going warrior of the arm-chair type, Thomas sauntered over and had a confab with Stanton, who delayed for time, to send a message to Capitol Hill. To his side now swarmed a group of fighting, squabbling Radicals from both the Senate and the House! One and all itched to give some sort of battle to Andy Johnson. Charles Sumner, too squeamish to show up in person, sent him a fight-provoking message, which contained the one word "Stick!"

In a bar that night and later on at a fancy-dress ball,

General Thomas was the stellar constellation. Excited newsmen, politicians, army men, and diplomats crowded around him to proffer advice and ask for his plans. "What did he propose to do?" the crowd asked him. "Break down the door and assume my lawful post!" bragged the doughty old warrior, made strong and unafraid by frequent libations.

The following morning, aroused from his drunken slumbers, Thomas was confronted by Marshals, bearing an order of arrest signed by Judge Carter and asked for by Secretary Stanton. Haggard, peevish, and fight-provoked, the appointee went to court and posted bond for his appearance. It is a matter of record that he asked Judge Carter if the order for his arrest prevented him from finding Stanton and having things out with him! Assured that it did not, Thomas hurried to the White House and talked things over with Andrew Johnson. The President, as one can well imagine, was thumping mad. "I'm glad this has happened as it has," he informed Thomas. "Now we can have the Tenure-of-Office Act settled in the courts. The moment you are arrested we will take out a writ of habeas corpus and that will end the matter."

Encouraged, the General sauntered across the street and tackled Stanton again, demanding that he leave the office and building. A crowd gathered to see the fun, consisting mostly of Radical Members of Congress. If the onlookers expected bloodshed, they were quickly disappointed, for Stanton sent a messenger across the street to a saloon for a bottle of whiskey and soon the men were drinking toasts to each other by the brimming tumblerful![180]

As can be imagined, the country was in an uproar when they learned through the press what was happening in Washington. Johnson was almost snowed under by telegrams and letters of approval, but more than one such well-wisher scolded him for not having acted sooner. Ever since the execution of Lincoln's murderers, an ugly rumor had floated over the country that Johnson was afraid to demand Stanton's resignation because the little Secretary knew "too many inside facts." All too many men felt the Tailor's greatest weakness was procrastination. They didn't

127

realize that his slowness to act was merely his judicial mind studying all the angles involved.

On Capitol Hill, excited, belligerent men could talk of nothing but the need to teach Andy Johnson a lesson he would never forget. Resolutions were hurriedly passed, disapproving of his actions in removing Stanton. Johnson promptly vetoed them and, in ringing words, challenged Congress to do what it liked, "regardless of personal consequences to myself."

John Covode, of Pennsylvania, immediately introduced an impeachment resolution when Johnson's veto was read. Two hours later, the Reconstruction Committee, whipped into a frenzy of spleen by Thaddeus Stevens, passed recommendations of impeachment charges, alleging that Andrew Johnson was guilty of high crimes and misdemeanors in office. Two days later, after bitter debate, during which the outnumbered Democrats tried desperately to defend their leader, the Covode resolution was passed by a vote of 126 to 47. The vote was purely a party one. Not a single Democrat voted "yes" and not one Republican voted "no." The following day, Stevens and Bingham appeared before the Senate to advise them of the action of the House.

Johnson's efforts to test out the legality of the Tenure-of-Office Act in the courts came to dismal failure through the cunning of the Radicals. While the House was debating Covode's resolution, Thomas and his lawyers were lining up in Judge Carter's court. The General walked forward and demanded that he be placed under arrest and his lawyers were ready to sue out their writ of habeas corpus. Stanton's lawyers suddenly realized the plight their client would be in if this were permitted. Swiftly, they informed the court they were not asking for Thomas' arrest. Whereupon the judge promptly discharged the prisoner, thus ending the President's efforts to have the matter tried in the courts and not by Congress. In the War Department, learning of events, Stanton replenished his store of food and wine, determined to stay in the office until Congress had settled the matter for him. In the meanwhile, the whole Nation seethed and boiled over the affair. Only a few people knew the real truth about things. The great majority had to

128

believe, or disbelieve, what they read in the Radical-controlled press—that Andy Johnson was a villain and a traitor to the Nation and now his sins were finding him out.[181]

With all danger of a writ of habeas corpus and a court fight out of the way, Congress now felt free to get rid of Johnson in their own fashion. The Senate promptly concurred with the House on Covode's charges.[182] Seven managers were chosen to handle things—Bingham, Boutwell, Butler, Logan, Stevens, Williams, and Wilson. Hurriedly, eleven charges were drawn up against the President. The only reasonable charge was that he had violated the Tenure-of-Office Act. One article accused him of giving illegal advice to General Emory. Article Ten was the most laughable of all. In it he was charged with having incited the people "in a loud voice" during his Swing around the Circle tour to mistrust the good motives of Congress!

Years later, in his autobiography, Ben Butler makes this asinine confession: "I came to the conclusion to try the case [Impeachment] as I should try a horse case, and I knew how to do that." In all probability, it was this very spirit that defeated the Radical plans.

Working at top speed, highly elated and cocksure of themselves, the Radicals forced things through so fast that they quite forgot what thin ice their charges rested on. By midnight, March 4, 1868, all their plans were formulated. On the morrow at high noon, the Senate would hear the case for impeachment against the President. Salmon P. Chase, Chief Justice of the Supreme Court, would preside.

Various formalities delayed things day by day and it was not until March 23, that the actual trial was under way. The President, through his counsel, had asked for forty days in which to prepare his answer to the ludicrous charges. This the Senate refused to grant. Ten days were sufficient, they contended, after Ben Butler had sent them into gales of laughter with a quip that God had managed to destroy the world by flood in forty days, so why did Andrew Johnson need equal time?

In the meantime, strange, bizarre things were happening behind the scenes.[183] One of the President's trusted lawyers for his defense was Jeremiah Black, late Attorney General. Black, as we have stated earlier, was attorney for Patterson, Murguindo and Company, of Baltimore, claimants to the little guano island, Alta Vela, off Santo Domingo. The company, on March 6, assigned a one and one-half per cent of their interests in the island to Black and his law partners. In the very midst of preparations for the President's defense, Black went to Ben Butler, James G. Blaine, John A. Bingham, and W. K. Koontz and secured letters endorsing company claims to the island. He also received verbal opinions from Thaddeus Stevens, James A. Garfield, and several other leading Radicals.

Exactly what happened isn't very clear, but Johnson's Secretary, Colonel Moore, left shorthand notes[184] in his official record book that on the 12th of March, Black brazenly approached the President and showed him these letters, most of them dated March 9, after the trial had proceeded. With never a hesitation, he calmly asked approval of his client's claim to the island, linking the President's decision in the matter with the impeachment trial. He also left him a note, which read: "Unless you can do something for your friends, it is useless for me longer to apply my personal and professional powers where defeat stares us in the face.[185] The next day the papers quoted him as having told the President that he had no hopes for his acquittal.

Johnson listened to Black as calmly as he could. Then his temper got the better of him. Leaping to his feet, he cried out in great rage, "You try to force me to do a dishonorable act, contrary to the law and against my conscience, and rather than do your bidding, I'll suffer my right arm to be torn from the socket. Yes, quit! Just one more word—I regard you as a damned villain. Get out of my office, or, damn you! I'll kick you out!"

Black fled to take counsel with his partners and Radical conspirators on the Hill. They urged him to try and smooth things over. Accordingly, he wrote Johnson a letter of apology, but Johnson was angry and thoroughly disgusted. He ignored the letter, but he announced to the press, through Attorney General Stanbery, that Jeremiah Black was no longer connected with him. It made a news-

130

paper sensation, but Black instantly countered with a statement that he had dropped out of the case because he didn't think the President stood any chance of acquittal! Small wonder the public was bewildered. Small wonder, too, that they flocked into Washington from far and wide to attend Andy's trial. They packed the galleries, and a huge overflow that numbered many hundreds patiently stood out in the blustery, snowy park before the Capitol, waiting for news of the proceedings inside.

Time and again Chase had been obliged to remind frenzied Senators that there were certain rules of law and logic to which they must stick. Long recognized as a personal enemy of the President on Reconstruction policies, Chase nevertheless proved himself fair, impartial, and judicially indifferent to Radical threats and efforts at intimidation. He considered the trial impolitic and illegal.[186]

One interesting highlight should afford readers a clue to the caliber of the men who were so desperately seeking to tear the President down. Ben Wade, President of the Senate, would automatically have succeeded to the Presidency of the Nation if Johnson could be impeached and removed from office. Despite this fact, Wade was permitted to take an active part in the trial and to vote guilty, or not guilty, on all articles! It is a matter of record his vote was "Guilty!" throughout the proceedings. It is also a known fact he had been so assured of becoming Johnson's successor that he had tentatively selected his Cabinet officers.

Slowly, relentlessly, more damaging to the accusers than the accused, the trial dragged on while not only Washington but the whole land seethed and argued and fretted, and even girded itself for the possibility of a second Civil War. It was almost akin to a continuous Roman holiday, and when the daily bickering ended in the Senate, it lasted most of the night in the saloons, bawdy houses, social functions, and wherever else men gathered. Gideon Welles left his own broad interpretation of the trial: "The Constitution-breakers are passing condemnation on the law-supporter; the conspirators are sitting in judgment on the man who would not enter into their conspiracy, who was, and is, faithful to his oath, his country, the

131

Union and the Constitution. What a spectacle! And if successful, what a blow to free government! What a commentary on popular intelligence and public virtue!"

From the opening hour, the Radicals found themselves beaten in logic, cross-examination, and cold, merciless facts. It was apparent from the very start that the charges against Johnson were too forced and nonsensical to stand up. But, unwilling to admit defeat, the Radicals tried everything from trickery to intimidation and bribery. They whipped the entire country into partisanship in the fight. Legislatures, public mass meetings, lodges, fraternal groups, even church conventions were solicited to bring pressure against Senators whose final verdict was in doubt to the Radicals. Old Thad Stevens, more dead than alive, probably shortened his life in the frenzy of his forensic attacks against the Tailor. Time and again the galleries were the scene of organized demonstrations by Radical-inspired hoodlums. Some of these things were so vile, uncouth, and apparent that they sickened a few Senators who otherwise might have sided with Radicals.

In the White House, Andrew Johnson went on trying to do his work, while at the other end of the Avenue men screamed and shouted and struggled for the chance to tear him down and make his name a dishonored, blackened thing. Calmly, he interviewed callers, went on desperately with his efforts towards Reconstruction, gave several state dinners and even attended one or two outside dinner parties. He spent a great deal of time with the slowly fading but ever-courageous Eliza and his fearless and serenely poised daughter, Mrs. Patterson. Johnson didn't give a whoop what happened—whether he was impeached or not. Deep in his heart he knew he was right, and that was enough for him.

Came the fateful day, May 16, when Justice Chase called the roll on the question of guilty or not guilty. Men's hearts almost stopped beating as they waited for each man down on the floor to give the answer. It was on the question of the eleventh article, the article Old Thad had felt would do the trick if all else failed.

One by one the roll was called. "Guilty!" came from

132

thirty-five throats in various stages of emotion. "NOT GUILTY!" answered nineteen men, too resolute and honorable to be swept off their feet. One vote shy of the required two-thirds needed,[187] the amazed, chagrined, and beaten Radicals slunk from the chamber, while the jubilant Democrats and Conservatives rushed about in their frenzy of joy.

Colonel William Crooks, waiting in the rear for that final verdict, ran all the way from the Capitol to the White House with the happy tidings, disdaining a horse in his excitement. Spent, breathless, he staggered into the library, where Johnson sat talking with Secretary Welles and two other men, whose names Crooks did not know. "Mr. President!" he cried, wild with emotion, "you are acquitted!"

For a moment Johnson was calm, accepting the handclasps of everyone in the room. Then tears rolled down his face.[188] Crooks stared at him in stark disbelief. A butler appeared and the President righted himself. He ordered some whiskey and everyone present drank a silent toast to this amazing individual who had gone through so much for his country.

Suddenly the room filled with excited, noisy, and demonstrative friends who had arrived from the Capitol, hoping to be the first with the news. Johnson stared at them for a moment or two and then slipped upstairs to the bedroom where his wife lay propped up on the pillows.

Thad Stevens was like the fabled man who threw a boomerang, only to be hit by it himself. He had grown weaker and weaker during the last days of the trial and it was common talk that only his thirst for vengeance against the Executive kept him alive. He could no longer walk alone, and for weeks had been carried to and fro in a strange and clumsy makeshift sedan chair, held aloft by two husky Negro boys. He was constantly obliged to flag up his failing strength with drafts of brandy, a bottle of which was kept in open view on his desk. It was a dramatic moment for the gallery spectators when he poured himself a fresh draft and the old rogue made the most of it.

"This country is going to the devil!" he had cried out

when his much-vaunted eleventh article went down in defeat. The shock almost killed him, then and there, but thanks to his brandy bottle, he rallied to scheme some more. On the 7th of July, after the House had reconvened, he made the last public utterance of his life, and it would have been far, far better never expressed. In a great burst of passion, he had informed the startled House that because it seemed "impossible to remove an executive by peaceful means, the only recourse from tyranny would be Brutus' dagger!" He followed this ghastly tirade with a resolution offering extra reasons for impeachment—five of them, to be exact. But they were never acted upon. A few days later, he died in the arms of his faithful colored friend. For a day and a night, his body rested in state in the rotunda of the Capitol. Then it was removed to Lancaster and buried in a Negro cemetery—by his own wish. The faithful Lydia was handsomely remembered in his will (and a nephew might have been even more so, had he fulfilled the old reprobate's demands—that he abstain from the use of alcoholic beverages, which he was unable to do).

Thus passed from the national scene one of the most amazing and powerful figures ever to stand in the limelight.

One thing is sure—Stevens' fellow townsmen did not share his spleen against the President. One of the congratulatory telegrams he received on acquittal read: "Ten thousand hearts are throbbing with exultations of joy. Justice has triumphed over party," and it had been filed from Lancaster! Citizens of other cities were as lavish in their effusions and congratulations. Many held torchlight processions and others fired salutes from one hundred guns. From faraway France and England came cables of confidence.[189]

Andrew Johnson had won.

CHAPTER 15

PRAY FOR ROME

Although it was natural that Johnson would have liked the nomination of the Democratic Convention that summer, the trial and the verbal fireworks had so split the country that it was deemed unwise. The choice went to Horatio Seymour, who never had a chance running against such an opponent as Grant, who was backed by almost limitless money.

From John Quincy Adams, II, grandson of John Adams, there came to the Tailor a letter so fine that we quote it in full here. Adams had lost the election to the legislature of Massachusetts because he had dared back the President. Now he had recently won the nomination for Governor on the Democratic platform. The letter is dated September 23, 1868.

> I believe that those men who like yourself can dare to grasp great eventual gain to their country at the cost of a temporary disfavor to themselves are doing as noble a work as men can do. My grandfather used to predict that when the great slavery struggle which he saw pending closed, [it would be high time] for calm and patriotic men to be gathering around the organic law.
>
> When that day comes, and come, I am convinced it will, when that great paper is once more cherished as the most precious possession of the people; and these clouds which gather now so black are rolled away, no name will be entitled to higher place, and no fame worthy of a brighter page in our history than that of the President, who dared alone to set his face against the momentary madness of the myriad and at the risk of all that is dearest to a public man, defend it to the bitter end, and Ark of the Convenant intrusted to his faithful keeping.[190]

In our discovery of the Adams letter, we found in the same issue of *Century* an article by Major Benjamin C.

Truman, who had served as Johnson's Secretary during his military governorship in Tennessee. Truman became a special agent of the Post Office and during the trial was located on the Pacific Coast. He wrote Johnson his congratulations on his acquittal, and in answer, Johnson wrote him one of the longest letters he probably ever penned to any man, telling him of his difficulties. What makes it of great interest is what he had to say about Grant.

> Grant was untrue. He meant well for the first two years, and much that I did that was denounced was through his advice. He was the strongest man of all in the support of my policy for a long while and did the best he could for nearly two years in strengthening my hands against the adversaries of constitutional government. But Grant saw the Radical writing on the wall, and heeded it. I did not see it, or, if seeing it, did not heed it. Grant did the proper thing to save Grant, but it pretty nearly ruined me.

There are many other things in this intimate letter to Truman that give a clear picture of the real Johnson. Evidently Truman had said something to him about General Miller, whom he appointed as Collector of the Port of San Francisco. "I have received a number of letters from General Miller, explaining that in denouncing my policy of Reconstruction he meant no personal reflection on me. You may say to General Miller that on account of his distinguished services in Tennessee during the war, nothing that he can say about me will affect my esteem for him; and also say to him that so long as I am President of the United States, he shall be Collector of the Port of San Francisco."[191]

In the same letter there are some tremendously interesting comments on famous men of the day. He compared Horace Greeley to a "whale on shore"—always floundering and "He nearly bothered Mr. Lincoln's life out of him and it was difficult to tell whether he wanted Union or separation, war or peace. He is all heart and no head . . . the most vacillating man in the country." Evidently Blair had begged Johnson to add Greeley to his Cabinet. In this letter the Tailor wrote: "I told him that Greeley was a sublime old child and would be of no service to me at all."

Perhaps the most startling sentence in this letter is where he analyzed his views of Union Generals. "Grant has treated me badly; but he was the right man in the right place during the war, and no matter what his faults were, or are, the whole world can never write him down—remember that!" The letter closed with Johnson's comments on the rebel leaders. He reiterated his belief that treason should be made odious and that Jeff Davis and a few others should be hanged for the good blood they spilled on both sides. "But I might lose my head, for Horace Greeley, who made haste to bail out Jeff Davis, declares that I am a traitor. Just think of it."

Johnson's last year in the White House was not one continuous, drawn-out round of bickering and quarrels. Business and statecraft went on as usual, and almost endless were the details. Johnson's staff worked to the state of exhaustion, and in driving them on, he never spared himself. The end of the war brought on a myriad of problems. The nation had to change its gears from the business of slaughter to the gentler meshes of peacetime. There were great financial problems to meet and the currency and bond questions were vexatious.[192]

Johnson's unhappy administration was faced with sadly troublesome foreign affairs. Mexico was like a cocklebur in the bed of state. England and France and Spain agreed on a joint military operation against the turbulent and peppery people below the Rio Grande. These nations sent warships and transports loaded with troops to take possession. This was a violation of the Monroe Doctrine and the stage was all set for destructive explosives. Time and again, hotheads clamored for war with England, even while we were in the thickest of internal warfare among ourselves. Getting France out of Mexico and starting the reparation claims against England for her aid to the Confederacy took a great deal of time. Grant did his best to get Johnson to declare war against France immediately following the close of the Civil War. Johnson steered a course of peace.[193]

The purchase of Alaska was a murky affair and its successful ending is due solely to Johnson and Seward and the Russian Ambassador who crossed Radical palms. Johnson and Seward also arranged for the purchase of the Island of St. Thomas for the Navy, but the Radicals blocked the plan. Had it gone through, it is improbable we would have been obliged to declare war on Spain towards the end of the century.

Constantly in the background, great scandals in railroad grants, gold manipulations, and whiskey tax thefts cropped up to embarrass Johnson. The perpetrators were Radicals, and although he not only tried to fire them and also to prosecute them, he was powerless because Congress stood in his way.

In the South, things were gradually growing worse as the stricken people tried to carry on under bayonet rule. The Carpetbagger was having his day and, slowly but surely, what was left of the riches of the South found its way into the coffers of the North. In June, 1868, however, Johnson was enabled to issue a proclamation that told the world all the southern states were now reunited with the Union—even though the reuniting method wasn't his idea of real Reconstruction.

Stanton had resigned immediately after the Impeachment trial. After considerable trouble, Johnson finally got the Senate to approve of General Schofield as his successor. Thereafter no further trouble issued from that former festering place. The Senate, however, refused to confirm Johnson's appointment of Stanbery to his old post of Attorney General. He was rejected on the grounds he had acted as "counsel to the great criminal!" Finally, through the intervention of friends, Johnson asked that the place be given to William Evarts, and this was accepted.

In the election of 1868, Grant proved an easy winner. The tension continued to grow between the two men and neither would finally see the other. The last break came on New Year's when, against his will, Johnson invited his successor to the annual reception. Grant didn't answer—instead, he left town.

As March neared, Mrs. Patterson began to give the White House one of the most thorough house-cleanings it had ever received. She began the sad task of private possessions

138

being shipped back home. There were thousands of last-minute visitors, all anxious to say good-by. A delegation from Baltimore composed one group of callers begging Johnson to spend a week in that city as a civic guest before he left for Tennessee. Touched, the Tailor said yes.

Johnson was so thoroughly disgusted with Grant that he refused to attend his inaugural! Scores of people begged and pleaded with him, but the Tailor stood like granite in his refusal. They suggested two separate parades, but the President declined to attend, as did the two Adamses at the inauguration of their successors.[194]

It must have been a strange, awkward last hour there in the White House. Until the very last moment, Johnson was signing official papers and dictating final memos on the status of things for the benefit of his despised successor. Promptly on the stroke of noon, he climbed into a carriage and departed.

The departure of the Johnson family from the White House was notable for two things, and the first was so unusual that not only Secret Service made note of the fact, but the servants gossiped about it and the press was moved to reluctant admiration: There was no procession of drays and express wagons carrying away priceless gifts such as usually marks the exit of a late Chief Executive.

There is only a record of small gifts, such as some wine from old friends, home-ground meal from home, and a few inexpensive things the children had received.

These things, however, came from old and tested friends, too well acquainted with him to have their offerings looked upon as bribes for favors to come. Indignantly, Johnson had spurned gifts of blooded horses, silver-plate, steamer tickets around the world, and a host of other things less impeccable men accepted, and still accept as the prerogative of their high office. His departure in this respect was so unusual that Senator Doolittle made it the subject for a speech in the Senate on March 4, 1869.[195]

A farewell message marked the end of Johnson's incumbency—a sort of recountal of his stewardship of the Nation's highest office. Even as Grant was taking his oath and clearing his throat to make an inaugural address, Capitol news telegraphers were clicking off Johnson's caustic, ironic message to the papers of the world.

The servants of the people, in high places, have betrayed their trusts for personal and party purposes. While public attention has been constantly turned to the past and expiated sins of the South, these servants . . . have broken their oaths of obedience to the Constitution and undermined the very foundation of liberty, justice and good government. When the rebellion was being suppressed by the volunteered services of patriot soldiers amid the dangers of the battlefield, these men crept without questions into place and power in the national councils. After all danger had passed, when no armed foe remained, when a punished and repentant people lowered their heads to the flag and renewed their allegiance to the government of the United States, then it was that these pretended patriots appeared before the nation and began to prate about the thousands of lives and millions of treasure sacrificed in the suppression of the Rebellion. They have since persistently sought to inflame the prejudices engendered between the sections, to retard the restoration of peace and harmony, and by every means, to keep open and exposed to the poisonous breath of party passion, the terrible wounds of a four year war. They have prevented the return of peace and the restoration of the Union and in every way, rendered delusive the purposes, promises and pledges by which the army was marshalled, treason rebuked and rebellion crushed, and made the liberties of the people and the rights and powers of the President objects of common attack. They have attempted to place the President under the power of a bold, defiant and treacherous Cabinet officer. They have robbed the Executive of the prerogative of pardon, rendered null and void acts of clemency granted to thousands of persons under the provisions of the Constitution, and committed gross usurpations by legislative attempts to exercise this power in favor of party adherents. They have conspired to change the system of our Government by preferring charges against the President in the form of articles of impeachment, and contemplating, before hearing or trial, that he should be placed under arrest, held in durance, and, when it became their pleasure, to pronounce his sentence, driven from place and power in disgrace.

Mincing no words and sparing nobody, the intrepid, dauntless Tailor went on to describe the lawless, unconstitutional acts whereby Congress had betrayed the people for purposes of selfish gain. "Conscription, confiscation and

140

loss of personal liberty, subjection of states to military rule, the disfranchisement of whites and the enfranchisement of blacks for party purposes were only a few of the things he pointed out. His final words gave the Nation something to think about:

> They have in time of peace increased the national debt by a reckless expenditure of the public moneys, and thus added to the burdens which already weigh upon the people. They have permitted the nation to suffer the evils of a deranged currency, to the enhancement in prices of all the necessaries of life. They have maintained a large standing army, for the enforcement of their methods of oppression. They have engaged in class legislation, and built up and encouraged monopolies that the few might be enriched at the expense of the many. They have failed to act on important treaties, thereby endangering our present peaceful relations with foreign powers.[196]

The Radical party press frothed and thundered at the temerity of a runaway tailor's apprentice speaking about his betters. *Harper's Weekly* caricatured him as an obese merchant, peddling secondhand clothes. But the Democratic papers were stricken with some form of repentance. For days, they filled their columns with glowing eulogies.

From the White House, the Johnson family went to the home of John Coyle, one of the publishers of the *National Intelligencer,* there to spend a week or so while the womenfolk bought furnishings for the Greeneville home, to which abode their thoughts were happily returning. Idle for years, and having been used by both opposing armies for everything from a brothel for colored soldiers to a hospital for wounded officers, it had suffered badly from neglect. Johnson had not seen the place for eight long and bitter years. Now, suddenly free of public office for the first time in over thirty years, he found himself yearning for it as never before. He was tired and weary and he wanted a little period of peace while he could think out things. His battle for the people wasn't won yet, and nobody realized it better than himself.

On March 12, 1869, Johnson paid his promised visit to Baltimore as a guest of that city.[197] Accompanied by a retinue of friends, his special train pulled into the Camden

Street Station to find a vast horde of people excitedly awaiting him. The platform was crowded with distinguished people. Outside, a band played military airs and a cavalry escort, as well as a battery of field artillery, stood about an open carriage, drawn by four dappled horses. Down the streets went the procession through great crowds of shouting men, women, and children. Overhead, in every block and stretching from building to building, were banners eulogizing his greatness and eloquently bespeaking Baltimore's appreciation for his courage.

It was perhaps the greatest ovation ever given him and, for once, emotion overcame him. For three long hours, he stood in the Post Office rotunda and shook hands with endless rows of people. That evening he was guest of honor at a lavish banquet in the old Barnum Hotel. The toasts they paid him were partial compensation for all that he had gone through for the Nation. "Future generations will impeach his impeachers and find them guilty, not this distinguished patriot!" cried one civic dignitary, while banqueters roared their approval.[198]

He was flushed and happy by the warmth and sincerity of his welcome. He wrote his daughter that he loved Washington even where so many of his foes still wore the masks of deceit and sham friendship.[199] But there were those whose sincerity and genuine affection for him left no room for doubt, and to these he turned in the few days remaining for him in Washington—faithful old Gideon Welles, Seward, Coyle, and a few of the Senators. These pressed him for a statement regarding his future plans, but he laughed and shook his head. All he could think of was a return to the hills and peaks of eastern Tennessee he loved and hungered for so much. Perhaps, like the psalmist of old, he wanted to look up to them for strength enough to meet the last battle of his life.

CHAPTER 16

UNCONQUERED AND UNCONQUERABLE

March 18 witnessed the departure of the Johnsons for home. As their train neared the Volunteer state border, the Tailor's courage gained new strength by the presence of cheering crowds along the route, who demanded his presence on the platform. At Bristol there was an unexpected reception in the depot as the little party was changing to a special train. A happy crowd demanded a speech and the Tailor found it impossible to refuse—especially when the mob begged him to become the state's next Governor![200] The rest of their journey home was like a triumphant procession. At every village and town, the engineer stopped the train and made the welkin ring with bell and whistle while the excited inhabitants crowded along the tracks and cheered for "Our Andy!" Small wonder happy tears trickled down the seamed face of the homesick warrior. These were his own people, and yonder against the skyline were the hills of home!

Greeneville was in gala attire when the train finally pulled into the station. A band blared and voices roared huzzas of welcome. Triumphantly, the whole population streamed after his carriage to the old brick house on the sloping street, which he hadn't seen in eight long years. Again and again, they begged him for a speech, and from the porch he finally mastered his emotion long enough to express his thanks and to briefly tell of the terrible years and the sufferings he had undergone for the sake of the people.

How different his last sight of town! Regarded as a traitor then, today they found him a public hero! Greeneville did its best to hold the worn and scarred warrior in their midst, but as well try to corral the wind or capture fog and rain. A few days of absolute rest from matters of

143

state—utterly happy days, in which he roamed the streets and chatted with one and all, renewing old friendships and bridging the gaps left by the years—and the Tailor had made up his mind!

He wanted vindication from the world at large! He wanted the whole Nation to realize that he had been right from the start of his administration and that the Radicals had been dead-wrong. But how best to do this wasn't instantly clear to him. He was still physically young, having barely passed his sixty-second birthday. His health was fair and his vigor was unimpaired. There was a spring in his step and he possessed boundless energy.

Late in March, Johnson was inveigled into coming to Knoxville, where an audience of five thousand people were awaiting him. The pleadings of dozens of men had brought about the trip. There was a procession of importunate citizens who insisted and begged that he help bring the state and the Nation out of chaos. To the wildly cheering Knoxvillians, Johnson declared that his life's ambitions had been satisfied "BUT, it is natural that I desire to set my policies right before you and not be so badly misunderstood."

Back in Greeneville again, he did some thinking. Already the Grant administration was dropping its mask of sanctity, and honest citizens were viewing with alarm the start of a carnival of unbridled graft. Johnson made no bones about his hatred for Grant. He knew the sycophants about him and he knew the Nation was utterly at the mercy of unscrupulous men. Every decent instinct in his soul bade him act for the Nation before it was too late.

Johnson set forth on a speaking tour of the state. From the mountains to the muddy Mississippi, he rode in a special train, making speeches wherever a crowd would gather. That was no problem. The problem was mostly to make his voice ring out to the farthest edges of the great gatherings who enthusiastically turned out at news of his arrival. The Radicals in the state were alarmed and their fears were echoed in Washington. This man who set such store by the Constitution must be shut up—but how!

On August 2 at Maryville they used a mob to break up

144

Johnson's speech.[201] Nothing worked. The Old Warrior was too smart. In ringing, plain words he told the people of his beloved state that they were in the hands of unprincipled thieves and that something must be done about it. June found him back in Washington again, watching his youngest son graduate from school. There he startled the newsmen who hastened to visit him with a statement that "Grant did not understand a single great national issue and that he was mendacious, cunning and treacherous. He lied to me, by God! and I convicted him before my whole Cabinet!"[202]

On his return to Tennessee, Johnson threw his eloquence into the gubernatorial race then in progress, on the side of D. W. C. Senter, the incumbent, who was a bitter foe of the Radical Party. This maneuver gave a clue to his plans: If Senter was re-elected, Johnson could hope for election to the U. S. Senate, the moment a vacancy occurred! The possibility so alarmed his foes that they were prepared to stop the Tailor at any cost. Even President Grant wired leaders on the subject, and to one visiting state Radical, he said bluntly that "he would regard Johnson's election to the Senate as a personal insult to himself!"[203]

That October, Johnson's name was put in nomination for the senatorship, the motion being made by State Senator Edmund Cooper, formerly one of Johnson's Secretaries. The Radicals spent money like water to buy opposing votes, and in their despair, Johnson's friends did a little offering themselves to buy the two votes necessary for him to win. Johnson heard about it and insisted the deal be called off. His friends protested, whereupon the Tailor calmly said: "All right! Go ahead! If I'm elected by purchased votes, as sure as the Lord lets me live, I'll go before the Legislature and expose the deal and refuse the office!"[204] That ended the matter, but it brought about a queer situation—Henry Cooper, brother of Johnson's own political manager, was elected in a move by the Radicals and a few conservatives, who blindly hated Johnson, receiving fifty-five votes to Johnson's fifty-one. It was mortifying to Edmund Cooper; he was not to blame. It had been planned in a Radical caucus in Cooper's absence. Johnson never found out about it. To his grave, he felt he had been cheated by those he had trusted and his enmity towards the Coopers became an open affair.

For the next few years, Johnson sought unceasingly for a chance to return to Washington, either as Representative or Senator—wanting to stand among his enemies again and fight with them on even terms. But those enemies were wilily alert and the whole national Radical movement entered the Tennessee hustings to thrust him back whenever they could.

When the terrible cholera epidemic swept through Tennessee in 1873, it was hoped that the ex-President would flee to a place of safety with his family, as he was well able to afford such a departure. Stubbornly, however, he refused to desert his fellows, and the outcome was that he came down a victim to the scourge himself. It was the worst illness the Tailor had ever experienced in his life, and, for days, he lay at death's door. Finally, he recovered, but gone was the buoyant strength that had so amazed friends and foes alike. His heart especially suffered, but, nevertheless, his fighting spirit swept him on.

Perhaps one reason for his renewed struggle was the sudden failure of the bank wherein he had deposited his principal lifesavings, the First National Bank of Washington. When it closed its doors, it was indebted to Johnson for $73,000. It was a hard blow, and the Tailor must have been tormented by the thoughts that he and his family might end their days in poverty. He hurried to Washington to study the situation at firsthand. What he discovered, revolted and sickened him, but gave him new fighting courage.

All that year, the Nation had rocked with one sickening scandal after another, emanating from Washington and involving many of the most prominent politicians in the land.[205] There had been the whiskey ring, land steals, bond steals, Indian Department frauds, and whatnot. The speculations in gold had been the most scandalous of all, with men like Jay Cooke, James Fiske, and Jay Gould suddenly exposed as merciless rogues, who, by bribery and graft, had actually used the United States Treasury in the hopeless ignorance of Grant to ruin rival speculators, as well as thousands of smaller investors.

Then came the infamous Credit Mobilier[206] exposure. This was a syndicate formed to take over the building of the Union Pacific Railroad and it had for its sole purpose the looting of the stockholders by excessive charges for materials and construction. Through bankruptcy proceedings, the thieves meant to exhaust the resources of the parent company, in which they were the principal stockholders, and then seize control through legal trickery. To carry out their nefarious plans, they had liberally issued free stock to most of the Administration leaders and other key figures in and about Congress. It was bribery, pure and simple, and when exposure came, there in the hideous limelight stood all the party leaders from the Vice-President down—Patterson, Boutwell, James A. Garfield, Dawes, Bingham, Pig-Iron Kelley, Allison, Wilson, Schofield, and Brooks, et al. Most of these men had been Johnson's bitterest enemies, the Vice-President, infamous "Smiler" Colfax, worst of all.

For months, investigation succeeded investigation, with the newspapers divided as ever in their allegiance to party and belief of "guilt," while the taxpayers held their breaths and wondered. There came a day when the investigating committees turned in their final reports, and as was to be expected, whitewash was the order of the day, with one or two of their less-valued members being tossed to the "lions" of justice. It is interesting to record that Thomas Nast had been bribed to spring to the defense of the guilty Congressmen by making cartoons against newspapermen who denounced the villains too forcibly and strenuously for comfort. One of these cartoons had a caption reading "Let him who has not betrayed the trust of the people and is without stain cast the first stone!" The subject was Justice pointing a stern finger to crouched newspapermen labeled by their famous names! Obviously, the public could not help but thereafter question the honesty of such prominent writers as Dana, Bennett, Reid, Watterson, and several others.

Scarcely had the stench of the Credit Mobilier floated

away when the famous Banking House of Cooke collapsed, with a crash that was heard around the world. Financial angel of the Radical Party, Cooke is famous in history as the man who financed the Civil War through his sales of national bonds. With the New York Branch closing first, and the Washington First National following within a matter of moments, there was nothing for the main establishment at Philadelphia to do but follow suit. Pandemonium swept across the Nation like a prairie fire. Cooke and his agents had sold hundreds of millions of dollars of not only government bonds, but other investments as well, and their dazed creditors numbered into the thousands, including widowed washwomen to the Nation's financial giants.

Overnight, scores of the biggest firms in America were obliged to suspend business because of the Cooke crash. Several days later, the great banking firm of Henry Clews & Company failed to open its doors. Grant and Secretary Richardson, of the Treasury, hurried to New York in a desperate effort to stave off the collapse of their political empire, so largely built on fraud and loot.

With these failures, came dreadful exposures of corruption and betrayal of public trust. The Grant Administration had carried huge accounts with the Cooke banks, and despite the national banking law, these deposits had not been legally protected. The evidence proved that the Cookes had partly operated on Government money, loaned to them without security! How a thing like this "escaped" the eyes of National Bank Examiners was easily explained. Almost every Radical in Congress owed money to the Cookes in the shape of generous "loans" of various sorts! Thus, they had bought protection from audits and had managed to put over some of the greatest steals in our whole history! There are several interesting biographies of the Cooke family available to readers, but in the pages of those volumes, one finds nothing but eulogy for a pair of shrewd financiers. To get the truth about them, one must search the newspapers and magazines of that day.

Johnson, hurrying into Washington to see what he could do about his own seventy-three thousand dollar deposit, learned many things. What seemed to anger him most was that when failure became evident, Henry Cooke had fore-warned Grant and other leading Radicals to withdraw their own deposits in time to prevent loss. The night of October 17, 1873, several thousand anxious men gathered in the street before the Metropolitan Hotel and shouted them-selves hoarse for a speech from Andy Johnson. From a balcony, he gave them a short one that spared no man's reputation who he felt was implicated in the scandals of the day. The Nation, reading of what he said in their papers next day, remembered them at the polls, and the Radicals took a terrible beating for their sins.

Back in Tennessee again—hobbling about and saving his strength as best he could—the Tailor continued his travels up and down the state, telling of the evils of the Grant regime to anyone who would listen. People couldn't help but admire the scrappy old fighter, and had it been left to their own actions, would have swept him back into office again with their blessings.

"Whose ox have I taken?" he would roar out into a crowd, outlining his stewardship of public office. "I never took any gift and I challenge any man to prove otherwise!" Then he would give a list of all the things Grant was known to have accepted. To this he would give a list of the offices Grant had supposedly "sold" to party leaders.

But, convincing the people and fighting corrupt legis-latures were two different things, and 1873 closed with the Tailor still "in pasture" when all the while his spirit cried out to be back in harness again. It seemed his chance would never come; that his enemies were stronger than he.

In the fall of 1874, he was more determined than ever to return to the Senate. He sent his secretary, Colonel Reeves, to canvass the legislators and his report was gratifying. He then covered Tennessee from Bristol to the Mississippi attacking Brown as his most serious competitor. He de-nounced the Cooper brothers. At Columbus there were threats of assassination; speaking nevertheless, he turned this to his advantage. All to good effect—when the legis-lators met January 4, 1875, Johnson had ten more votes than his nearest competitor, and the supporters of Brown and Bates fought one another to a standstill, as shrewd

Andy had guessed. For four days the legislature locked in debate; every day saw Johnson gain more. On the fifty-fourth ballot, Johnson won over Parson Brownlow. He would at last return to the national scene.[207]

Now he was where he wanted to be once more, and God help his enemies! Perhaps it wasn't a charitable and Christian thought, but the fact remains, the Tailor seems to have felt himself a Scourge of God, returned to punish the lawless.

Not only Tennessee seethed with wild excitement that night of triumph—so did much of the rest of the Nation. In many cities throughout the country salutes of guns were fired in his honor and bands played to his memory. Editorials eulogizing him appeared in all the leading newspapers. The consensus of editorial thought was, "He had dug himself out of the deepest pit any politician had ever before fallen into!"

In Washington, there was an unhappy feeling among certain gentry who had dipped into the Pork Barrel too often and too long. They dreaded Johnson's tongue[208] and they dreaded his honesty. They knew that "easy times" were over now.

CHAPTER 17

CATO'S WARNINGS

Andrew Johnson took stock of himself as he stared thoughtfully out at the rolling landscape. The attack of cholera he had suffered in '73 had played hobs with him for a long while afterward, but the doctors assured him there had been no organic damage. He had no aches and no pains, but he knew full well the old vigor and spring were gone forever. His present uneasiness was less physical than it was mental—it seemed a vague sort of premonition or foreboding.

Action! Action—by God! That was what he wanted—action! He itched for that moment when he would stand up in the Senate again and get the chance to turn his verbal batteries against his old enemies and, thus, the enemies of the Nation.

It was March 4, 1875. The native ruler of the Sandwich Islands was making an official visit to Washington, and Grant was using his presence as an official excuse for a special session. The public was informed that it was for the purpose of treaties in the interests of trade and future naval security. But Andrew Johnson and many other men on the inside knew differently. Grant was in trouble over Louisiana, and he wanted the Radicals in the Senate to justify his plans for forcing that state to accept the despicable Kellogg for Governor again. His plan was so rotten it smelled to high heaven and Johnson planned to let the whole country know how he felt about the matter—especially Ulysses S. Grant!

Washington quickly spread the news that night: America's most famous "Comeback" was among them, registered in humble quarters at the Willard Hotel. Hundreds came to pay their respects, and more jammed the lobby and corridors just for a possible glimpse of the fighting Tennesseean who refused to give up.

Johnson minced no words in assuring his visitors that he had returned for the sole purpose of speaking out against the Grant Administration. The crowds cheered him lustily. He wasn't quite the old, vigorous, pugilistic leader but, if his body seemed less supple, his mind was as agile and logical as ever.

His oath-taking proved a great drawing card to politically-minded Washingtonians. They flocked to the Capitol and when the galleries were filled, the people packed the corridors and overflowed to the front of the building. Those fortunate enough to have seats were to be onlookers at a dramatic spectacle.

Deliberately arriving at the Senate a few moments late, Johnson walked slowly and sedately down towards the desk his ancient enemy, Brownlow, had abandoned. It was banked high with exquisite blooms of camellias—sent in his honor by young ladies who, as children, had been entertained by him at the White House. They had never forgotten his courtesy. At the sight of them, Johnson's composure nearly broke. At that moment the spectators identified him and a mighty roar of acclaim rolled down—a welcome so universal no one saw fit to check it.[209]

The moment found Edmunds, of Vermont, addressing the chair and the tumult overhead startled him, for nothing he had said deserved applause. Puzzled, he turned his head, and there, a few paces behind, stood the man he had once voted to expel and had castigated so unmercifully. His mouth sagged and his eyes quailed like those of a boy caught red-handed in the pantry. Johnson, aware of his feelings, stared at him with studied purpose. A scarlet flush spread over Edmunds' face and his body suddenly trembled like a person with ague. Someone tittered. Others took it up. Desperately, the Radical fought for self-control, but in vain. One hand went out to steady himself against his desk. It struck a pile of books and, as they clattered to the floor, Edmunds dropped weakly down to his chair. His conscience had suddenly caught up with him. For

152

a fleeting second he had been the focusing point for hundreds of all-seeing eyes.

His discomfiture seemed a sort of signal. With one simultaneous movement, almost every other Member on the floor rose to his feet in a signal of respect. A bevy of fellow-Democrats nearby sprang to Johnson's side to wring his hand and escort him the rest of the way. But the Old Warrior seemed not to see them. His eyes—those strangely magnetic orbs that had confounded so many men in the past —were sweeping all around the chamber, searching out his old friends—and enemies. How few of the old stalwarts were left now—the men who had stood by him during the darkest days of his life! And where, oh, where, were the Radicals who had wounded him so deeply in the past?

There was Sherman with a timid, apprehensive look on his face! The Senator faced him squarely. Sherman, fearful of a rebuff, moved up the aisle to Johnson's side. Awkwardly, he held out his hand, half-certain it would be rejected. A smile lighted his face as Johnson grasped it warmly. Morton, archenemy of all who were left, stood like a statue, bewilderment written on his face like a mile-high word. He saw Johnson smile at him, and instantly he had worked his way to his side with boyish agility. As their hands met, a little sigh of approval broke out from the standing ranks. Who said this man had come bent on vengeance? Why, this seemed like a reunion of old friends!

The writers of that day somehow forgot to tell us how Boutwell looked and acted. However, they left unforgettable pictures of how most of the others felt and acted. There was Frelinghuysen, notably. He grew so confused and agitated he fell to his knees and, when asked why, said he had dropped a paper under his desk!

It seemed as though many moments went by as Johnson stood there, but in reality the hands of the chamber clock had barely moved. Sometime later, surrounded by a group of elated friends, Johnson moved forward to take his oath of office. The rare spectacle of an ex-President in a new role was so great that the chamber buzzed and echoed with excitement. As Johnson faced the Speaker, every Member present rose to his feet and solemnly stood at attention. The brief ceremony over, a motion of adjournment followed almost immediately.

Later, in the cloakroom, Johnson held an impromptu reception. Men crowded about him, eager to shake his hand and put themselves right in his good graces. Johnson studied them with more than passing interest. Of the thirty-five Senators who had voted to expel him, only thirteen now remained. Justice, slowly but inexorably, had somehow eliminated twenty-two of them. Thad Stevens and Charles Sumner were dead; Ben Wade, Ben Butler, and a generous dozen others had met defeat at the hands of disgusted voters. In the cloakroom, when asked what his reactions were, Johnson replied with some emotion: "I miss my old friends—all are gone now but you, Senator McCreery!"[210]

For twenty days, Johnson sat in his seat and listened to the acrid debate for Senate approval of two resolutions which had been presented by Morton, of Indiana. One was to give Congressional sanction to military interference in the Louisiana elections, thus returning to office the deposed Radical Governor William Kellogg, whom irate citizens had finally repudiated. The other would have granted a seat to P. B. S. Pinchback, a Louisiana mulatto, over whom a controversy had raged for three long years.

Johnson had been in Washington but a few days when he sent a message to his old bodyguard, William H. Crooks, at the White House, to visit him some evening in his hotel room. Crooks, elated at the summons from his old Chief, lost no time. For a while, the two men sat and chatted of the old days. Johnson, in a reminiscent mood, told of the unhappy death of his last son, Robert, and of how his hopes were pinned now on his sturdy grandchildren. Finally, he arrived at the core of his summons.[211]

"Crooks," he said, "you pasted a lot of notices about Grant in my scrapbooks and you ought to remember where they are, for I don't. Here are the books. Please find them." He waved his hand to a corner, where stood a stack of scrapbooks. The Secret Service man plunged to the task, marking the various places with little slips of paper. As he rose to go, the ex-President waved him back to his chair.

"Crooks, I have come back to the Senate with two purposes. One is to do what I can to punish the southern brigadiers. They led the South into secession and they have never had their deserts. The other—" He paused and his face grew dark.

"What is the other, Mr. Johnson?"

"The other is to make a speech against Grant. And I am going to make it this session."

Crooks concluded his memorial of that last meeting with Johnson by alluding again to Johnson's capacity for hatred.[212]

On March 22, Johnson delivered his speech.[213] He undoubtedly made finer speeches in his long career than the one he made that day, but this one was so packed with things the people wanted some honest legislator to say at last. He had his own "axes to grind," it is true, but as he ground them, his auditors knew his ringing words were said for the whole country at large and not merely for Andrew Johnson. He wasn't an individual any longer— he was the heart and soul of the whole Nation, pleading, demanding, and insisting on justice, peace, and understanding without any further delay.

His entire audience broke forth in wild, tumultuous cheers as he struck at Grant. He didn't deliberately accuse Grant of graft, but there was little need to openly discuss what most people were thinking. By innuendo and references to history, he compared Grant with other men who had sold their honor and betrayed their trust for baubles and trinkets. The galleries whooped and cheered when he thundered forth the lines:

> Upon what meat doth this our Caesar feed
> that he is grown so great
> that he can prescribe and lay down
> empires and place commanders over them?

Condemning sometimes, castigating and pleading at others, Johnson carried his audience with him until the day waned and the gaslights were turned on. Breathlessly, the great audience sat there enthralled by his words, and among the Senators around him were dozens who heard in them the death knell of their hopes for a continuation of their

155

easy graft and the survival of the Republican Party as it flamboyantly existed at the moment.

Listening to him now, one and all knew that Grant had been duped. His minions had nothing but ulterior motives in their minds when they demanded that an ousted governor be forced back on the necks of an angry, indignant citizenry. They knew in a trice that there was something as odorous as ripe cheese behind the eagerness to seat Pinchback. Allow Grant to return for another four years? NO! NO! A thousand times no! The tumult in the galleries suddenly became so great the Speaker had to interrupt, demanding that extra guards be sent upstairs to maintain strict silence.

Swiftly and fiercely, Johnson pleaded for justice for the South, and all the Nation. He begged men to forget party and cliques and to stand humble and earnest around the Constitution.

It was almost over now; he was tiring fast and his audience leaned forward to better register his eloquent plea, their faces tense with emotion and ardent with quickened patriotism. Feverishly, and with fingers racing at top speed, the newsmen bent over their pads to jot down the flaming words that were destined to restore sane treatment to the South and defeat all of Grant's fond hopes for continued life at the White House. A final outburst utilized his old trick of inflaming his listeners with patriotic impulses. But different, indeed, were his closing words, for Johnson had suddenly grown very old and tired and such mundane and earthly things as party "lines" were erased forever from his mind—"Let us come up to this work forgetting what we have been heretofore. Let us lay aside our party feelings; let us lay aside our personalities and come up to the Constitution of our country and lay it upon an altar and all stand around, resolved that the Constitution shall be preserved."

So great the effect of his words upon the Senate that day that Members seeking the floor in the closing moments, ACTUALLY apologized for their presumption!

The people were aroused from their lethargy at last. The Radicals didn't need the flood of angry letters and

156

telegrams to learn that a national house-cleaning was now in order. Intuition told them that, the moment Andrew Johnson "said his piece" and sat down. They had been indicted, their shams and tricks exposed to the merciless light of reasoning and an entire Nation was about to pass verdict upon them. So, let Pinchback and Kellogg and their ilk and ken take care of themselves while they got out of their own predicaments!

The special session was over the next day. A treaty had been arranged with the King of the Sandwich Islands, but Grant had been toppled from his throne by a battered, tired, old warrior, who had asked for nothing else from life but vindication at the hands of both the people and his accusers.

He had won both, just as he knew he would. Again, he was a national hero with all the old papers and magazines that had so badly blasted, twitted, and smeared him, exhausting their stock words of eulogy. Of a truth, they cried, "Andy is the greatest patriot among us all!"

Never before had the Smokies lured Johnson in his thoughts as they did on the weary train ride home after the session had adjourned. He hungered fiercely for a sight of their rugged pinnacles against the sky, their tips wreathed in the lambent haze from which came their name. He seemed so very, very tired! If only he could fling himself down on the top of one of those peaks and just rest a while. A while? No—rest forever!

In Greeneville, people crowded around him to laud and bask in the emanations of his renewed national greatness. But it was a new sort of Andy who waved them aside. The old friendliness was gone, it seemed, and he was possessed of a mood approaching aloofness. But, he couldn't seem to get enough of the companionship of his wife and daughters and his adored grandchildren.

Andrew Johnson knew his day was spent. He knew it with the intuitive knowledge that possesses men who have learned to be introspective. His mind and heart were tired.

A few happy weeks with his family about him, then, on July 28, 1875, he boarded the train to Carter Station to spend a few days with his daughter, Mary Stover, and her

157

children. At luncheon that noon, he seemed happier and more vital than in many a day. A nap was suggested to him; he headed up the stairs to his room, gaily escorted by his little granddaughter, Lillian Stover. Lilly was eager for news of Washington and her amiable grandfather was full of stories she hungered to hear.

As she left his room, her little feet stopped short at the sound of a strange noise from the room she had just left. Calling back, she heard no answer, and with her curiosity aroused, returned to look within. What she saw brought a piercing scream to her lips. Grandfather had fallen to the floor—every muscle of his body locked in the rigors of paralysis. His face was mottled and there was a strange, tense look in his eyes.[214]

Stricken with horror, the child bent over him. "Grandfather!" she cried, "Are you hurt? Did you fall? Speak to me!" But Johnson couldn't speak. Desperately he struggled to form words, but the power to talk had gone. He couldn't hear Lilly's frantic questions. Help came quickly to get him into bed and it wasn't very long before the nearest doctor was bending over the rigid form.

That evening they brought Eliza from her own sickbed. Tears flowed thick and fast from the anxious visitors as they watched the silent greeting between these two whose attachment for each other had been such a magnificent and lasting thing. Near the end of her own life, Eliza knew death held no terrors for either of them. One pair in life, their religion had prepared them.

Desperately, the doctors worked over their inert patient. They saw in those hypnotic eyes of his how terribly much he wanted to talk before it was forever too late. Slowly, the long night passed, and with morning came a change for the better. "Prop me up, Doctor!" he gasped out suddenly. "There is something I want to say!" Amazed, they obeyed him and then hovered in the background as relatives and close friends clustered about the bed. With a strange vigor, Johnson jested and bantered with those about him, and as his voice flowed on and on, their hopes quickened that the end was still far away.

For hours, he chatted and reminisced the past. Like a panorama, his thoughts unrolled back to his youth and the struggle for foothold to his goal in life. Long-forgotten things flooded back into his mind and his listeners smiled as he remembered the old days. Perhaps the doctors should have made him keep quiet, but they didn't, and what followed was obvious—evening brought on a second stroke and his voice was forever stilled. There was still life in him, but it was flowing fast.

At two-thirty in the morning, July 31, 1875, Johnson died.

The news stunned the Nation.[215] All too late, an entire country seemed to waken to the fact their mightiest man had left them. From near and far came the dignitaries to pay their last respects. Down from the hills and coves of the Smokies poured Johnson's staunchest friends—the mountain men and their wives—by the thousands.

Through a town heavily draped in mourning went the hearse, followed by a single carriage bearing the feeble Eliza and her daughters. On foot, behind, came thousands of mourners, tears falling unashamed from their eyes, as they struggled up the hillside to the spot he had long ago marked for this very purpose.

He was not buried in an elegant coffin as people wanted it to be, but that didn't matter much. What did matter was that they carried out Andy's last wish—under his head they placed his worn and well-thumbed copy of the Constitution of the United States—and for a winding sheet they had wrapped him tenderly in the flag he had so devotedly served.

Sometime later at the dedication of the Johnson Memorial at Greeneville, there was present a small, beautiful young woman who had once lived in Nashville and now was the wife of a young Kentucky Captain. As she tossed her floral offering on the monument, she must have remembered that day back in 1865, when she had sworn a day would come when she would dance on this man's grave! Laura Carter had grown a woman at last. Ben Truman, Johnson's old Secretary, standing there, recognized her and in a flash, his mind went back to that long ago moment.[216] Thoughtfully, he stared across the valley at the

159

distant Smokies with their eternal haze. His staunch heart was filled with bitterness and grief. If only the Nation had known this man as he had, what troubles it might have been spared!

BRIEF BIOGRAPHICAL SKETCHES

B. CARROLL REECE, the author of *The Courageous Commoner,* was born at Butler, Tennessee, on December 22, 1889, and died in Washington, D. C., March 19, 1961. He was the son of John Isaac and Sarah E. (Maples) Reece.

He attended Carson and Newman College, 1910-14, New York University, 1915-16, University of London, 1919; he received the honorary degree of LL.D. from Cumberland College in 1928, Tusculum College; H.H.D., Lincoln Memorial University, 1946.

Mr. Reece married Louise Despard Goff, October 30, 1923, and had one daughter, Louise Goff (wife of George W. Marthens II, Colonel, USAF).

He served as assistant secretary and instructor in economics, New York University, 1916-17; director School of Commerce, Accounts and Finance, New York University, instructor economics (day division), 1919-20.

Mr. Reece was chairman of the board of Carter County Bank, First Peoples Bank of Johnson City, Kingsport National Bank, Farmers Bank of Blountville. He was publisher of the *Bristol Herald Courier.*

Mr. Reece was elected to Congress in 1920 as the baby Member, and he served from the 67th Congress into the 87th Congress. This was the longest service of any man from the First Tennessee District in its history. At his death he was on the House Rules Committee, a committee that is the most powerful in Congress. He was a member of the special House Committee on Postwar Economic Policy and Planning, and served as chairman of the special Committee to Investigate Tax Exempt Foundations. From 1940 on, Mr. Reece was Republican National Committeeman and state chairman for Tennessee. He was chairman of the Republican National Committee from April, 1946, through July, 1949.

He served as Regent of the Smithsonian Institution in Washington. He was president of the Robert A. Taft Memorial Foundation, and vice-president of the American

Good Government Society and a member of the Institute of Political and Fiscal Affairs.

Mr. Reece enlisted in the United States Army in May, 1917. He was commissioned a Lieutenant of Infantry in August, 1917. He served with the 26th Division, American Expeditionary Force, from October, 1917, to July, 1919. He was commander of the Third Battalion, 102nd Infantry. He was decorated with the Distinguished Service Cross, Distinguished Service Medal, Purple Heart, and the French Croix de Guerre with palm. He was cited for bravery by Marshal Philippe Petain and Generals Edwards, Hale, and Lewis.

Mr. Reece was a member of the American Economic Association, American Statistical Association, American Academy of Political Science, American, Tennessee, and District of Columbia Bar Associations.

Mr. Reece was a Baptist; Mason (32nd Degree, Shriner). He was a member of the Metropolitan Club, Capitol Hill Club (president), Chevy Chase Club, Burning Tree Club (Washington), Lotos (N.Y.C.), Johnson City (Tennessee) Country Club.

Below are the citations he received when he was awarded the Distinguished Service Cross and the Distinguished Service Medal:

Distinguished Service Cross

Carroll Reece, First Lieutenant, 102nd Infantry, 26th Division, in Bois-d'Ormont, France, October 23-28, 1918. In leading his company through four successful actions, he was twice thrown violently to the ground and rendered unconscious by bursting shells, but upon recovering consciousness he immediately reorganized his scattered command and consolidated his position.

On several occasions under heavy enemy machine gun fire, he crawled far in advance of his front line and rescued wounded men who had taken refuge in shell holes.

Distinguished Service Medal

Carroll Reece, First Lieutenant Infantry, U. S. Army. He showed energy, initiative, and military ability of a high order while serving as Second Lieutenant in the 102nd Infantry, 26th Division, in command of a company and later a battalion.

He led his company brilliantly in the attack upon the St.

162

Mihiel salient, and during the operations of the 26th Division north of Verdun. Confronted later by a task of great difficulty when placed in command of a battalion which suffered heavy casualties and became badly disorganized, he displayed marked ability and determination in reorganizing his command and molding it into a good fighting unit, able under his leadership to achieve valuable results.

MRS. CARROLL (Louise Goff) REECE, congresswoman, was born in Milwaukee, Wisconsin, on November 6, 1898. She was the daughter of Guy Despard and Louise (Van Nortwick) Goff. She graduated from Milwaukee-Downer Seminary and Miss Spence's School, New York City. She married Congressman Carroll Reece, October 30, 1923. They had one daughter, Louise Goff (Mrs. George W. Marthens II).

Mrs. Reece is manager of the Goff Properties in Clarksburg, West Virginia. She is vice-chairman of the Board of Directors, First Peoples Bank, Johnson City, Tennessee, and Carter County Bank, Elizabethton, Tennessee; vice-chairman of the Board, Southeastern Security Life Insurance Company; Trustee, Taft Memorial Foundation, and Institute of Political and Fiscal Education. She is a member of the 87th Congress (First District of Tennessee). She served as a delegate to the Republican National Convention in 1956. She is a member of the Tennessee Historical Society, Business and Professional Women's Club, DAR, Colonial Dames, and Daughters of 1812.

Mrs. Reece is a member of the Monday Club, Johnson City Country Club, Chevy Chase Club, Capitol Hill Club, and Sulgrave Club (Washington).

Her home is at 1315 S. Roan Street, Johnson City, Tennessee. Office: House Office Building, Washington 25, D. C.

NOTES AND REFERENCES

CHAPTER 1

1. William Crooks, *Memoirs of the White House* (Boston, 1911), pp. 43-73; Margaret Spaulding Gerry "Andrew Johnson in the White House," [Memoirs of William Crooks] *Century*, LXXVI (Oct., 1908), pp. 653-669; 863-877.
2. Schouler, *History of the United States 1783-1877* (7 Vol.; New York, 1913), VII; Hall, *Andrew Johnson: Military Governor of Tennessee* (Princeton, 1916). Winston, *Andrew Johnson: Plebeian and Patriot* (New York, 1928). Milton, *The Age of Hate* (New York, 1930).

CHAPTER 2

3. James Schouler, *History of the United States* (7 Vol.; New York), VII, 142.
4. Robert W. Winston, *Andrew Johnson, Plebeian and Patriot* (New York, 1928), pp. 3-25.
5. *Ibid.*
6. O. P. Temple, *Notable Men of Tennessee* (New York, 1912), pp. 357-368; 360-363.
7. *Greeneville Sentinel*, Feb. 10, 1910; Gabriel Roquie, *A President's Love Affair*," *National Magazine*, VI, (April, 1897), 63-67.
8. James S. Jones, *Life of Andrew Johnson* (Greeneville, Tennessee, 1901), pp. 17-18.
9. *Ibid.*, pp. 18-19.
10. Johnson, Mss.; Milton, *Age of Hate*, p. 76; Gaillard Hunt, "The President's Defense," *Century*, LXXV (Jan., 1913), 425-426.
11. *Ibid.*
12. Temple, *Notable Men*, pp. 363-368.
13. *Ibid.*, pp. 369-382.
14. Mss., Johnson.
15. Temple, *Notable Men*, pp. 377-382.
16. W. M. Caskey, "The First Administration of Governor Andrew Johnson," *East Tennessee Historical Society's Publications*, I (1929) pp. 43-45. Caskey, "The Second Administration. . . ." *loc. cit.*, II (1930), pp. 34-54.

CHAPTER 3

17. *Congressional Globe.*
18. *Congressional Globe.*
19. *Congressional Globe.*
20. The Library of Congress has kept a record of his book withdrawals. In preparation of this speech he seems to have made liberal use of Wheeler's *History of North Carolina*; Holmes's *American Loyalists*, and Haywood's *History of Tennessee*. His speech also shows a profound knowledge of early history, the letters of James Madison and a wide survey of anti-slavery laws, and census figures and whatnot. Evidently he had spent many weeks in preparation.
21. *Life and Speeches of Andrew Johnson*, Frank Moore, ed. (Boston, 1865), pp. 82-84.
22. *Ibid.*, pp. 77-175.
23. *Congressional Globe.*
24. Moore, *op. cit.*
25. *Congressional Globe.*
26. Johnson, Mss.

CHAPTER 4

27. George F. Milton, *The Age of Hate*, p. 101.
28. Hall, *Andrew Johnson, Military Governor*, pp. 1-3.
29. *Ibid.*, pp. 1-5.
30. For Buchanan's cabinet, Allan Nevins, *The Emergence of Lincoln*, (2 Vol. New York, 1950), II *passim* and pp. 344-347.
31. Moore, *Speeches*, pp. 176-315.
32. *Ibid.*
33. *Ibid.*
34. Milton, *Age of Hate*, pp. 105-107.
35. *Ibid.*
36. Johnson Mss., L. C., Vol. 94, No. 10,912.
37. Milton, *Age of Hate, loc. cit.*
38. W. G. Brownlow, *Sketches of the Rise . . . of Secession* (Philadelphia, 1862); *Parson Brownlow and the Unionists of East Tennessee* (New York, 1862).
39. Hall, *op. cit.*, pp. 14-17.
40. Johnson Mss., Vol. 18, Nos. 4104A, 4104C, 4104D.
41. *Ibid.*

CHAPTER 5

42. Truman, "Anecdotes of Andrew Johnson," *Century*, LXXXV, p. 436.
43. *Congressional Globe.*
44. Johnson Mss.

45. Johnson Mss. contain a volume of letters, proclamations, and speeches of Johnson as military governor. A kind of scrapbook, apparently kept by Johnson, newspaper clippings are also included. Much of what is said here of Johnson's public life as governor had this valuable volume as its source.
46. *Ibid.* See also Oliver P. Temple, *East Tennessee and the Civil War* (Cincinnati, 1899), pp. 163, 181, 183, 184, 189, 197, 536-539, for a contemporary political explanation of the situation in East Tennessee.
47. *Ibid.*
48. *O.R.* series, I, Vol. XX, Part II, Series I, XVI, Part II, 118, 119, 122, 159, 651, 658, *et passim*, C. R. Hall, *Andrew Johnson, Military Governor of Tennessee,* pp. 53, 58, 60-67.
49. Temple, *Notable Men,* pp. 400-422.
50. Johnson Mss., Vol. 30, No. 6689.
51. Winston, *Andrew Johnson,* p. 248.
52. *Ibid.*
53. *O.R.,* series 3, serial 125, IV, 1221.
54. *Ibid.*
55. Johnson Mss., No. 4944.
56. Hall, *op. cit.,* pp. 180-186.
57. Hall, *op. cit.,* pp. 91-94; *O.R.,* series 1, Vol. XX, Part II, p. 317.
58. Temple, *East Tennessee and the Civil War,* pp. 478-479.

CHAPTER 6

59. James F. Rhodes, *History of the United States,* (N. Y., 1928) IV, 517-526; 527-538.
60. Honore Wiltse, *With Malice Toward None,* (New York, 1928), p. 62.
61. Milton, *Age of Hate,* p. 31. Benjamin Butler, "Vice Presidential Politics of '61," *North American Review,* CXLI (Oct., 1885), pp. 330-334.
62. Adam Gurowski, *Diary.*
63. Rhodes, *History of the United States,* IV, pp. 520-531.
64. Milton, *Age of Hate,* pp. 40-58.
65. Blaine, *Twenty Years,* I, p. 522.
66. James F. Glonek, "Lincoln, Johnson, and the Baltimore Ticket," *The Abraham Lincoln Quarterly,* VI, (March, 1951) pp. 255-271: Glonek ably takes up the question of Lincoln's choice of Johnson, maintaining that Lincoln wanted the convention open. However, Glonek fails to weigh Lincoln's examination of Johnson by Gen. Sickles and lightly sets aside the need for a war democrat. The article, however, presents the infighting of the convention very well, particularly the reason for New York's final selection of Johnson, instead of the native Dickenson.
67. J. G. Randall, *Lincoln the President* (New York, 1955), pp. 132-134. For a good recounting of the election of 1864, see Chapter VII.
68. Alexander McClure, *Lincoln and the Men of War Times.*
69. Winston, *Andrew Johnson: Plebeian and Patriot,* pp. 261, 275.
70. Jones, *Life of Andrew Johnson,* p. 128.
71. Milton, *The Age of Hate,* p. 132.
72. Hall, *op. cit.,* pp. 139-156.
73. *Ibid.*
74. Yet, they were expectant of trouble, the abolitionist and Radical G. W. Julian considered Johnson a Negro hater and Southerner at heart and was disappointed in his nomination. *Political Recollections 1840 to 1872* (Chicago, 1884), p. 243.
75. Johnson Mss., Vol. 45, No. 4021; Vol. 57, No. 2434. James Schouler, *History of the United States* (7 Vol.; New York, 1913), VII, 7-9. *Diary of Gideon Welles* (3 Vol.; Boston and New York, 1911), II, 251-252. Hugh McCulloch, *Men and Measures of Half a Century* (New York, 1888), 373-374. Truman, "Anecdotes," *loc. cit.,* 437-438.

CHAPTER 7

76. Farwell's Mss. "memoirs" are at the Wisconsin State Historical Society. Photostat copies are in the Library of Congress.
77. *Ibid.*
78. *Ibid.:* see also Milton, *The Age of Hate,* pp. 160-161, Jones, *Johnson,* p. 136.
79. Theodore Roscoe, *The Web of Conspiracy* (Englewood Cliffs, N. J., 1959) implicates Stanton in the plot to kill Lincoln.
80. Richard Taylor, *Destruction and Reconstruction* (New York, 1955), p. 295.
81. See *Diary of G. Welles* for a meeting (April 16) concerning reconstruction, p. 291. For Welles's account of the events of April 14 and after, pp. 283-292.
82. Edward L. Pierce, *Memoirs and Letters of Charles Sumner,* 4 Vol. (Boston, 1893), IV, 196 ff.

CHAPTER 8

83. Claude Bowers, *The Tragic Era* (Cambridge, 1929), 242 *et passim*.
84. Welles, *Diary,* II, 289.
85. W. A. Dunning, *Reconstruction Political and Economic* (New York, 1933), pp. 36-37.
86. Crooks, *Through Five Administrations* (New York, 1907), pp. 84-85.
87. *National Intelligencer,* June 19, 1865.
88. Albert Bushnell Hart, *Salmon P. Chase* (Boston, 1899), pp. 334-340.

89. Walter L. Fleming, *Documentary History of Reconstruction* (2 Vol., Cleveland, 1906), I, 9-24.
90. For example, see "The Condition of Virginia—Its Wants," in the *Daily National Intelligencer*, June 10, 1865.
91. *Ibid.*, I, 77-78. See also: Dunning, *Reconstruction*, pp. 3-18; 203-219. W. L. Fleming, *Sequel to Appomattox* (New Haven, 1919); Johnson's Remarks, *National Intelligencer*, June 19, 1865.
92. *Ibid.*
93. *National Intelligencer*, 1865; Claude Bowers, *The Tragic Era*, pp. 200-201.

CHAPTER 9

94. *The Tragic Era*, p. v.
95. Matthew Josephson, *The Robber Barons* (New York, 1934); V. L. Parrington, *Main Currents in American Thought the Beginnings of Critical Realism in America*, III (New York, 1930), "The Great Barbeque."
96. Edward McPherson, *Political History . . . during . . . Reconstruction* (Washington, 1875), p. 141.
97. A. B. Paine, *Thomas Nast* (New York, 1904), pp. 106-117.
98. *McClellan's Own Story* (New York, 1887), pp. 151-152.
99. Fletcher Pratt, *Stanton: Lincoln's Secretary of War* (New York, 1953), is a favorable but very much mistaken view of Stanton. D. M. DeWitt, *The Impeachment and Trial of Andrew Johnson* (New York, 1903), contains a criticism of Stanton.
100. Ben Ames Williams, *Mr. Secretary* (New York, 1940). Roscoe, *The Web of Conspiracy*. David Miller DeWitt, *The Impeachment and Trial of Andrew Johnson* (New York, 1903), pp. 241-287, is very critical of Stanton.
101. Moorfield Story, *Charles Sumner* (Boston, 1900).
102. Bowers, *Tragic Era*, pp. 332-336. McCulloch, *Men and Measures*, pp. 232-234.
103. Samuel McCalt, *Thaddeus Stevens* (Boston, 1889).
104. See Allan Nevins in *DAB*. Ralph Korngold writes a favorable biography of him in *Thaddeus Stevens: A Being Darkly Wise and Rudely Great* (New York, 1955). I. A. Woodburn, *The Life of Thaddeus Stevens* (Indianapolis, 1913).

CHAPTER 10

105. Nicolay and Hay, *Lincoln*, IX, 104-109.
106. Henry Steele Commager, *Documents of American History* (New York, 1944), I, pp. 436-438.
107. *Ibid.* Milton, *The Age of Hate*, p. 126.
108. *Galaxy Magazine*, XIII (1872), 526 *et passim*.
109. Edmund G. Ross, *History of the Impeachment of Andrew Johnson*, (privately published, 1896), p. 17.

CHAPTER 11

110. E. P. Oberholtzer, *History of the United States Since the Civil War* (5 Vols., New York, 1917-36), I, 26, 192, *et passim*. Dunning, *Reconstruction*, Ch. IX.
111. Winston, *Johnson*, p. 307.
112. *Ibid.*
113. *Ibid.*
114. J. G. Randall, *The Civil War and Reconstruction* (New York, 1937), pp. 708-714, 718.
115. J. F. Rhodes, *History of United States*, VI, pp. 37-39.
116. Quoted in Walter Lynwood Fleming, *The Sequel of Appomattox* (New Haven, 1919), pp. 29-30.
117. *Ibid.*, p. 28. Fleming, *Documentary History*, I, pp. 142-143.
118. Also A. B. Hart, *Salmon P. Chase* (Boston, 1899), pp. 334-340; *DAB*, IV, p. 32.
119. Fleming, *Documentary History*, I, pp. 154-158, *et passim*. Johnson Mss.
120. *Diary*, II, p. 369.
121. See *National Intelligencer*, June 22, 1865.
122. E. M. Coulter, *The South During Reconstruction* (Baton Rouge, 1947), p. 34. Fleming, *Documentary History*, I, p. 117.
123. *John Sherman's Recollections of Forty Years . . .* (New York, 1896).
124. William B. Hesseltine, *Ulysses S. Grant: Politician* (New York, 1958), pp. 64, 66, 81.
125. Dunning, *Reconstruction*, pp. 54-59. E. P. Oberholtzer, *History of the United States Since the Civil War* (5 Vol., New York, 1917-36), pp. 124-131. Oberholtzer, however, takes his examples from the harshest states.
126. E. Merton Coulter, *The South During Reconstruction* (Baton Rouge, 1947), pp. 29-30.
127. "Report of Carl Schurz, on the States of South Carolina, Georgia, Alabama, Mississippi, and Louisiana." Executive Document 2, 39 Congress, 1st Session, p. 107.

CHAPTER 12

128. *New York Tribune*, October 14, 1865.
129. Howard K. Beale, *The Critical Year* (New York, 1931).
130. Library of Congress.
131. Blaine, *Twenty Years*, II, pp. 112-113, 126. *Congressional Globe*, 39 Congress, 1 session. Bowers, *Tragic Era*, ch. V.
132. *Ibid.*

133. *Ibid.*
134. James D. Richardson, *Messages and Papers of the Presidents*, 10 Vol. (Washington, 1897), VI, pp. 353-371.
135. *Journal of the Committee of Fifteen on Reconstruction*, ed. by B. B. Kendrick. *Columbia University Studies in History, Economics, and Public Law*, LXII (New York, 1914), pp. 221-264.
136. *Ibid.*
137. Johnson Mss. Speech, April 18, 1866.
138. Dunning, *Reconstruction*, pp. 30-34; 60-61.
139. *Messages and Papers*, VI, pp. 398-405.
140. Welles, *Diary*, II, pp. 434-435.
141. *Ibid.*, pp. 443-444.

CHAPTER 13

142. Welles, *Diary*, II, p. 454.
143. *Ibid.*
144. Schouler, *History of U. S.*, VII, pp. 61-64.
145. *Ibid.*, pp. 463-464; Richardson, *Messages and Papers*, VI, 405 ff.
146. Welles, *Diary*, II, pp. 463-464. Rhodes, *History of the United States*, VI, pp. 66-68.
147. Richardson, *Messages and Papers*, VI, p. 413 ff.
148. *Ibid.*, p. 417.
149. *Ibid.*, p. 413 ff.
150. Joseph Blias James, *The Framing of the Fourteenth Amendment* (Urbana, 1956).
151. Eric L. McKitrick, *Andrew Johnson and Reconstruction* (Chicago, 1960), pp. 326-355.
152. House Report, 39 Congress 2 session No. 16, "Report of the New Orleans Riots." This is of course a Radical document. See also Bowers, *op. cit.*, pp. 127-130. Welles, *Diary*, II, pp. 569-570.
153. *Ibid.*
154. McKitrick, *op. cit.*, pp. 421-447.
155. See: P. V. Nasby [David Ross Locke], *Swingin' Round the Circle* (Boston, 1867).
156. Beale, *The Critical Year*, Welles, *Diary*, II, pp. 529-535; 543-545; 571-581.
157. McKitrick, *op. cit.* Welles, *Diary*, II, pp. 553, 563, 577; On Removal of Stanton, pp. 582-583.
158. Welles, *Diary*, II, 588-596.
159. Gregg Phifer, "Andrew Johnson Delivers His Argument," *Tennessee Historical Quarterly*, XI (September, 1952), pp. 213; 212-234. See also (June, 1952) pp. 148-170.
160. *Ibid.*, pp. 593-594.
161. *Ibid.*, pp. 591-592. McKitrick, *op. cit.*, p. 428. note 21.
162. Alberg, "The New York Press and Andrew Johnson," *loc. cit.*, pp. 404-416.
163. Gregg Phifer, "Andrew Johnson Loses His Battle," *Tennessee Historical Quarterly*, XI (December, 1952), pp. 291-328.

CHAPTER 14

164. Welles, *Diary*, II, pp. 34-76. Richardson, *Messages and Papers*, VI.
165. See also William A. Dunning, *Paying for Alaska* (New York, 1912).
166. *Ibid.*
167. David Miller DeWitt, *The Impeachment and Trial of Andrew Johnson* (New York, 1903), pp. 138-139.
168. *Ibid.*, *passim.*
169. *Ibid.*, pp. 142 ff.
170. *Ibid.*, pp. 154-179.
171. Blaine, *Twenty Years*, II, pp. 342-347.
172. *Congressional Globe*, 40 Congress, 1st Session.
173. Johnson Mss., Vol. 108, No. 14, p. 342.
174. DeWitt, *Trial*, pp. 214-216.
175. D. M. DeWitt, *The Judicial Murder of Mary E. Surratt* (Baltimore, 1895); *Trial of John H. Surratt* (Washington, 1867).
176. Hesseltine, *Grant*, pp. 70-88, 105.
177. *Ibid.*, pp. 106-107.
178. Welles, *Diary*, III, ch. LVI.
179. Gus A. Crenson, "Andrew Johnson and Edwin Stanton . . . 1866-1868," Master's Thesis, Georgetown University (Washington, 1949).
180. DeWitt, *Impeachment*, pp. 353-356.
181. DeWitt, *Impeachment*.
182. *Trial of Andrew Johnson*, B. P. Poore, ed. (Washington, 1868).
183. Autobiography, p. 929; L. P. Stryker, *Andrew Johnson* (New York, 1936), p. 589.
184. Moore, *Transcripts*.
185. Milton, *Age of Hate*, pp. 534-539.
186. Hart, *Chase*, pp. 357-361.
187. Edmund G. Ross, *History of the Impeachment of Andrew Johnson* (Sante Fe, 1896).
188. Crooks, *Memoirs of the White House*.
189. Johnson Mss.

CHAPTER 15

190. *Century Magazine*, LXXV (January, 1913). Hunt, "The President's Defense."
191. *Ibid.* Truman, "Anecdotes."
192. Rhodes, *History of the United States*, VI, pp. 316-347.
193. E. P. Oberholtzer, *History of the United States Since the Civil War* (New York, 1917-36), I, pp. 510-516.
194. Welles, *Diary*, III, pp. 536-538.
195. *Congressional Globe.*
196. See Winston, *Johnson*, pp. 485 *passim*, for the farewell address and Johnson's homecoming.
197. Jones, *Johnson*, pp. 334-335.
198. Johnson Mss.
199. *Ibid.*

CHAPTER 16

200. Milton, *op. cit.*, ch. XXVI.
201. Milton, *op. cit.*, p. 657.
202. *N. Y. Herald*, June 27, 1869.
203. Milton, *op. cit.*, pp. 657-658; Johnson Mss.
204. L. P. Stryker, *Andrew Johnson* (New York, 1936), p. 831.
205. See Hesseltine, *Grant*, pp. 375 *et passim*.
206. Rhodes, *History U. S.*, VII, pp. 65-87.
207. Temple, *op. cit.*, pp. 440-441; Milton, *op. cit.*, pp. 662-669.
208. Oliver Perry Temple claims that he had promised the Republicans not to scourge Grant if elected, but this was one pledge he had no intention of keeping—not when the national interest was at stake. Temple, p. 442.

CHAPTER 17

209. Winston, *op. cit.*, pp. 503-505; also Julius Chambers, "From the Presidency to the Senate," *Harper's Weekly*, XLVIII (September 3, 1904), pp. 1356-1357.
210. Crooks, *Through Five Administrations*, pp. 149-151. See Winston, *op. cit.*
211. *Ibid.*, pp. 151-152.
212. *Ibid.*
213. Jones, *Johnson*, pp. 354 ff. *Evening Star*, March 22, 1875.
214. Winston, *op. cit.*, pp. 506-508.
215. See *Evening Star* (Washington) July 31, 1875, August 2, 3, 4, 1875.
216. Truman, "Anecdotes of Andrew Johnson," *Century*, LXXXV, pp. 436-437.

Attention: Mary Jane Fuller
The Promus Companies
1023 Cherry
Memphis, TN 38117